From the

C000120644

... a grace-fi

> To my wife Sue and my son Sam. We have already travelled many roads and have seen his grace. Who knows what God will yet do? The adventure continues! The best is yet to be!

With blessings from

300leaders.org   jubileechurchlondon.org

Mike Betts

Lastword Publications
Lowestoft, Suffolk, UK
www.lastwordpublications.com

First published 2010, by Lastword Publications
www.lastwordpublications.com
Lastword Publications works with authors and musicians,
businesses and charities to provide professional results
with maximum impact.

ISBN 978-0-9559439-5-9

Useful website links:
www.lowestoftcommunitychurch.co.uk
www.newfrontierstogether.org
www.relationalmission.com

Biblical quotations are taken from the ESV
© 2008 by Crossway Bibles.

Design and production by The Upper Room 020 8406 1010

Foreword

I have never attempted to write a book before. The idea and momentum arise more from my conviction about the concepts and principles than it does to my desire to be an author.

I have had the privilege over my Christian life to be exposed to some wonderful teaching and people who have lived out what I heard preached. Through learning the truths taught to me I have tried to shape my life in response to them and continue to do so. A foundation of knowing who I am in Christ and what he has done for me is without doubt the place from which everything else in the Christian life flows. Knowing the truth should and does result in a desire and pursuit of God and his purposes.

Others may have written much more eloquently than me on many of the themes I touch on. Praise God where that is the case. Nevertheless, I wanted to put into print some of the things that I believe can radically shape a person's walk with God, enabling him or her to be fruitful. It is thrilling to think that someone who comes after me might benefit from what I have learnt. I love the truths in Scripture about God's grace and the effect on people's lives when applied. It certainly seemed worth making some contribution to magnifying such liberating grace.

I have some huge debts of gratitude in getting this book ready. Phil Stoddart has taken my first thoughts and ideas and helped craft them into something much better than where they started. Phil, your tireless work on this book and your patience with me are not only unusual but deeply appreciated. You kept me going with this and I am glad you did.

Phil started Lastword Publications as a ministry that seeks to encourage emerging Christian writers, artists, musicians to develop the gifts God has given them and to make their influence greater than might have been the case on their own. Phil and his wife Heather are without doubt two of the people I admire most in life. They are heroes of the faith. They have faced huge personal challenges and yet instead of turning from God they have cast themselves on him. With all of their frailty, at times strongly felt, they have chosen to trust and obey him. They have found the Saviour and his grace in ways many people do not have to, and are living proof of much of what I have tried to write about. This book would not be here without them.

Special thanks go to David and Sarah Porter and Geoff Stevens for their hard work and skills in helping to craft the very raw product. I also want to acknowledge some of the wonderful teaching I have received and in particular, Terry Virgo. I have been surrounded and inspired by many people who handle the word with great accuracy. If I can just pass onto a new generation a little something, a small contribution to help them as I have been helped, then it will have been worth writing this book.

Introduction

"Many Christians are hindered from serving God, not because they are ungifted, unwilling or lack opportunity, but because they do not understand grace."

On the morning before I started writing in earnest, the hairdresser cut my ear! The less than mortal wound attracted a variety of responses from onlookers, ranging from apathy and mild concern to barely concealed amusement. The wound got me thinking about the reason for writing theology in an understandable, digestible way. I am convinced that a similar kind of cut has been applied to the Christian church, especially in the West. The cut may not be seen as mortal or serious; however, if left unattended the steady, slow dripping away of blood is relentless. It will gradually seep away power, health and ultimately, life itself, from the body. Truth has been severed, sometimes through clumsy hands and unintentionally, but often, with a deliberate mutilation in mind.

Jesus helped people grasp profound theological truths by using daily objects, routines of their lives, simple illustrations and stories. He tackled head on what righteousness means and how to be made righteous in God's sight. One illustration in particular concerned the difference between the heart and the flesh. In Matthew 23:26, Jesus exclaimed: *'You blind Pharisee! First clean the inside of the cup and the plate, that the outside also may be clean'.*

In no uncertain terms, the Pharisees were being confronted about appearing outwardly religious in order to be regarded as 'Godly people'. Jesus saw through this sham and challenged them: yes, live externally righteous lives, but also be righteous internally. Anything less is fundamentally flawed, as a supernatural heart-change wrought from heaven must occur for righteousness. We know that we have experienced this dramatic change, by evidence of it outworked in and through our daily lives. Jesus himself said: *'you will recognize them by their fruits'.* (Matthew 7:16)

This book is an outworking and exploration of what Jesus meant by his illustration of the cup or bowl being clean or dirty on the inside and outside. Grasping the principles behind this illustration can liberate and free all mankind from striving to be righteous by our own efforts. Failure to understand and apply the illustration produces misery and bondage.

My aim is to give Christian believers confidence that they can become everything God wants them to be in life and serve him. They can be motivated and secure in their aspirations because of who they already are 'in Christ' and because of what God has already done by the Holy Spirit. In short, salvation can now be worked 'from the inside out'. This liberating truth lies at the heart of Jesus' comments to the Pharisees as he observed them trying to please God through external acts. They hoped to affect the way God viewed them 'from the outside in'.

But we know God will view us … **From the inside out**.

Contents

PART
ONE

UNDERSTANDING

1 *Where do I stand with God?*

So glum and so gloomy
I stare into the mirror,
Consider the dismal failure.
Penetrate my eyes,
See behind the flesh
Help me understand misery

I see it everywhere I go. It's written in wrinkles on the faces of individuals so wanting to please God, but fatigued with the effort. It's stamped onto the corporate lives of churches, entrenched deep in their DNA and paraded in their services, clubs and housegroups. Many people I meet seem to have little or no understanding as to where they stand with God regarding judgment. Just how much of our salvation is his work on our behalf making us acceptable to him and how much is for us to achieve or maintain through works of righteousness?

This huge double-barrelled question can burden believers' hearts, leaving them unsure of their fundamental position in Christ. How much substitution for sin did God provide by the cross? Does it cover the things we continue to do wrong as Christians or is it limited to a one-off transaction that took place when we first believed, but now has to be regularly topped-up like a 'pay-as-you-go' phone tariff? If it did, then just as we fall out of favour with the mobile phone service provider until more credit is obtained, then so is the case with God. We sin and he's angry, we repent and he's happy. Up and down goes his demeanour according to our behaviour, leaving us never quite sure of where we stand.

Once we have accepted Christ into our lives, surely it shouldn't be that difficult to live and grow in accordance with the new life received? Isn't the desire to please God enough to sustain us as we battle against the flesh? Sadly our well-intentioned desire can be crippled by not embracing fully the truths of our new relationship with the Lord God. Many of us are hindered from serving him, not because of being ungifted, unwilling or unable to find opportunity. What often holds us back is fear and uncertainty, eating away like cancer and causing considerable damage.

Although the walk with Jesus has begun, there are certain aspects of the truth of God that have penetrated the head but fallen short of flowing through the heart. Does this sound like a familiar experience? Something enters our mind and worries our conscience. With troubled hearts we desperately fumble through the Bible looking for a verse that helps. And even if we find one that really should apply, somehow it doesn't go from head to heart if we are not convinced it is personally true for us.

From head to heart

Jesus said: 'You will know the truth and the truth will set you free'. Further study of his teachings will reveal that this was no invitation to become a bookworm, where the accumulation of knowledge eventually results in liberation. Rather he meant that knowing the truth deep inside the heart with firm belief will transform a person's life.

If you feel unwell and go to the doctor, you'll probably receive a prescription for some medication. Hopefully, the idea of swallowing the prescription will not occur to you, for it is only the medicine that will soothe your troubles. The paper note serves only to get what is needed. The Bible is a prescription and memorising a mountain of scriptures means nothing if the truth of them does not seep into your heart. There, they shape and direct your mind, your will and your emotions, informing your decisions and beliefs.

The Bible says that a Christian is dead to sin and alive to God and that he reigns in life through Christ. A simple yet heartfelt commitment of faith expressed at conversion is evidence of God's Spirit bringing someone to life. The heart was desperate to love and please God and the believer now starts from a place of being made righteous by and through Christ. This position is not maintained through his works or efforts and it is not possible for this to be undone. He is a 'new creation' who has passed from death to life. Believers who are baptised in water, symbolically demonstrate the going down to death of their old selves, and rising in the new life God has opened for them.

Righteousness is a gift from God. Only once the wonder of the gift is grasped, can the problem of the flesh begin to be tackled with confidence and security. The flesh itself is not made righteous, as until Jesus comes we are not bodily redeemed. We still have appetites and desires that belong to our unredeemed flesh. These, though, can be defeated with increased consistency by us being empowered through the Spirit of God dwelling within us and through the security that the promises of God bring, so we can say 'no' to sin. We can resist temptation. The more we do this the less appetising sin becomes and the less habitual old patterns will remain.

A believer, therefore, needs to think and act in line with his new nature which is trying to break through into his daily life in all aspects. He needs to realise God is for him, loves him and is not disillusioned with him as he never had any illusions in the first place! God knows who and what each of was at our worst. That is why we need a saviour to do for us what we cannot do for ourselves. The power of this new nature helps the believer transform his life so he becomes the real God-given self rather than a struggler yearning for whatever he imagines he wants. Yet for many people, embarking on a new life of liberation is a difficult path.

Struggling with change

As people grow through childhood they are shaped by influences from their culture and popular thinking, by education, the media and the people around them. This moulding of life can be likened to a childlike understanding that the sun, stars and planets revolve around the earth; for we are led to believe that each of us individually is at the centre of life. We see the sun rise and fall each day and conclude it orbits around each of us separately! Everyone believes this phenomenon is unique to him alone; it looks and feels like truth from the observations of our own perspectives.

However, as we come to Christ and start to let his truth speak into our perception of reality and 'truth', we find our little lives are not the centres of our universe around which everything else revolves. Romans 12:2 tells us *'be transformed by the renewing of your minds'* and inasmuch as that starts to happen, the gravitational pull of scripture makes us aware that reality is not how it might look or feel. We are temporarily disorientated. All we had been told before we believed in Jesus, was fundamentally flawed. The reality is that God is the centre and we are not. God is now the hub: reality without the creator is no reality at all.

Sadly, some people have a genuine conversion but their perception struggles with the change. They do not take hold of truths and promises concerning the transformation of the heart into a new nature alive to God. They go through the Christian life constantly concerned with their flesh and appetites and assume that these are a reflection of their hearts before God.

They consider themselves to be dirty in heart and fall far short of even the standards they set themselves.

Trying harder only makes things worse as despair and disappointment destroy motivation. As a result, even more appetites of the flesh become appealing and recklessness sets in to allow for some relief from forever feeling so bad about themselves and God. Other Christians do not outwardly seem to struggle with such thoughts and temptations, so they conclude that it has all gone wrong if it was ever right at all. 'Am I even saved?' is a question they often consider. Over time they come to believe that God must have the same attitude of disappointment towards them as they do themselves.

Others meanwhile, misinterpret salvation and the provision of a righteous standing before God as a license to do whatever they want. They mistakenly believe that the standards of living required by God are lowered to zero, or to what can be comfortably managed. Being saved and cleansed by Christ's sacrifice means always being righteous. The logic follows that God does not expect or require any behaviour pattern in particular to reflect who they now are as Christians. In such a context, effectively: anything goes!

Setting rules

Sometimes a church can be heavily influenced by such confusion. Beneath the surface, silently brooding icebergs of concern remain unchallenged. But above the water, sharp tips can be seen in the various practices of church life as to what is correct and right Christian behaviour.

Rules appear, such as: 'in this church we do not drink alcohol' and 'in this church we would not encourage you to read fantasy books about magic'. Some prohibit the wearing of jewellery while others frown on the use of make-up. The point is that there seem to be many rules to steward Christian behaviour to conform to what is considered pleasing to God, and thereby making us acceptable or at least confident of being accepted.

Should church leaders be prescriptive, instructing people how to live in definite ways like these? Supposing someone approached a leader, as happened to me recently, and asked "Should I let my children read 'Harry Potter' books?"

Such a question requires a thorough theological perspective to answer. It seems simple, but a simple response may actually do a lot of damage. Sadly, in the interests of ease and simplicity, if not clarity and illumination, some churches have just said 'yes' or 'no'. However, all that is achieved with these unconsidered answers are enforced lists of 'do's' and 'don'ts', conveniently stuffed into the pockets of those asking the question. Even worse, an on-going lack of theological maturity is revealed in church leaders who respond this way. A theological foundation needs to be in place before answering whether it is acceptable for Christians to read Harry Potter books or not, the Twilight stories or any other of the huge amount of modern mystical, magical stories that seem appealing.

The truth is that if we give people rules, we produce legalists. They are proud legalists if they keep these rules: pride of course being a sin removes all benefit of keeping the rules. A failure to keep the rules condemns miserable believers. Their logical conclusion is that they are neither good Christians compared to others, nor are they loved by God as they have let him down and hurt his feelings.

Rules also then start to make us judge others so it has a corporate effect upon church life: factions, divisions and judgments of others start to form. So someone may think about the person next to them, 'Hey, you've read Harry Potter but I haven't! I'm not as dirty as you are.' But sadly oh yes you are, you're proud, which is arguably a worse sin, so you're more dirty!

Rules in the Christian life never helped anyone. Jesus said of the law, that although it is good it can never save anyone. Its purpose is to reveal sin, show us we need saving and lead us to Christ. Once Christians, we die to the law as our old life is crucified with Christ.

How do I know how to live then?

Some things in Scripture are crystal clear. If someone comes to me and asks: 'can I sleep with my boyfriend?', I respond by asking them what the Bible says. Those who know their scriptures confess that they shouldn't sleep with the boyfriend, so I reply: 'Well don't then!' I have not been asked a real question: the person is simply trying to avoid being bound by something he knows in his heart is right.

If another asks whether drinking alcohol is right, again I ask: 'what does scripture say?' This time the reply may be: 'well it doesn't really say'. My suggestion then is: "well do what Paul says: find out what pleases the Lord" (Eph 5:17). We help people mature by putting the responsibility on them to find out what pleases God. What will make your life clean on the outside to match the inside? What will please the Lord in the way that you live? That's why for some people alcohol is not a problem, but for others it's bad, as they don't know when to stop and their behaviour gets out of control. It may be different answers for different people, as on this, Scripture is not definitive. We have to say: 'find out what pleases the Lord', by which I don't mean find out what pleases the Lord by trying everything and finding 'Oh no; that didn't please him!'

We have to find out by searching Scripture, gleaning advice from maturer Christians; by seeking to walk in the Spirit and finding the mind of the Lord on any given matter; by recognising our own weaknesses and knowing our vulnerabilities. All of us have different vulnerabilities and things that tempt one person may not affect another. I do not smoke, but understand that the appeal of nicotine is so strong for some people that it blinds them to the damage it causes their health and wallets.

Find out what helps or hinders your walk with God. Paul spoke in Corinthians of those who could eat meat purchased cheaply from the idol-worship market and others who felt it was tainted because of its origin. For Paul it was for individuals to decide how it affected them. Indeed, Paul suggested that as we grow in maturity, some things which troubled our young consciences do not continue in the same strength.

I remember as a young Christian throwing my substantial record collection into a skip! So, would I encourage all new believers to do this? Well only if it's Barry Manilow!! I would have to insist on that as a service to society! Seriously though, of course I wouldn't do such a thing. For me at that time my life had been affected and shaped by the music culture around me. I wanted to express and distance myself from that influence. Now, however, many years later I can listen to the same music without it causing me a problem. I have matured in Christ; I am able to stand more securely in him without having to react to such things.

Some things are obviously wrong, for example, sexual immorality. It is clearly forbidden in Scripture and reading the Bible is how this is discovered. There are other things that are debatable. The reason I encourage each Christian to 'find out what pleases the Lord' is because Paul said 'I want to present every man mature in Christ'. In other words I want people to decide wisely about how they live without endlessly asking me what they should do!

Such a constant asker is not mature. He or she just wants a rulebook and that's not maturity. The correct approach is to hand the responsibility firmly back to the enquirer so that he decides whether to let children and young people read certain books, see particular films or play computer games that Christians have doubts about. Find out whether these things will be a problem or not. I won't tell him, because I want him to get to the point where what is in the heart – a clean and new nature - shapes what is lived out in his life.

Condition and position

If someone does enquire of their church leader whether a certain course of action and behaviour is appropriate, what do they think will be the consequence if they do approve but God does not? Would they be guilty again in their standing before God in terms of righteousness?

Believers often misunderstand the difference between their 'condition' and 'position'. If someone gets angry and swears due to provocation, they wonder how they now stand before God. If they say 'sorry', is it gone? Suppose they do it again? Why did they do it in the first place, as surely if they were clean inside something like this would not so easily happen?

It is important we understand that our position and condition are quite different concepts. While both are explored later in greater depth, our condition concerns our behaviour patterns born out in thought and deed. Our position is that once in Christ we are made righteous forever by his finished work. We are born again with a new heart and nature. The old has gone. We don't have to keep ourselves righteous forever by doing good works or keeping up some kind of standard that makes us continue to be accepted. What is more, not only are we clean now but there is provision for future sins, as an old hymn says:

"Here's pardon for transgressions past,
It matters not how black their cast;
And, O my soul, with wonder view,
For sins to come here's pardon too."

CH Spurgeon[1]

2 *Misconceptions*

I'm not sure of you Dad
You used to be angry
When I did those things
But now you don't seem to care.
Are they not really that bad
And what about me
Am I not guilty anymore?

Part of the perplexity that exists over our standing with God is to do with him! Is he consistent; does he get angry anymore? How does he feel when I mess up? I can well remember the early days of my Christian life. I had responded initially to the preaching of the gospel but was not sure I was saved. How could I know? I had prayed the right kind of prayer and felt as I should when praying it. How did I know how God felt about me: was he readily embracing me or did I have to achieve some greater standard before being acceptable? Six months of agony followed, so much so that at one point I genuinely felt I wished I had not heard the gospel at all. It seemed that not knowing was better than knowing; for the latter meant being unsure if I had a part in such a wonderful salvation. Why did I have such a bumpy introduction to the Christian life? Why was I not sure if I was saved in those early days?

My upbringing was in a Christian family. Although I can hardly remember anything about my father who died when I was seven: not his voice, nor anything he said or did, he still made a huge impression on me in terms of awareness of eternal things. I can remember my mother telling me the last thing he said before he died. He said to her: 'I will see you in the Glory'. I was so struck even at a young age how anyone could be so confident of their eternal destiny when facing imminent death. He knew his last breath here would merely mark a passing to a certain and real life in the eternal realm, at present hidden from our view until the renewal of all things removes the distinction.

His grasp of what was to come had grown from a long Christian life, lived learning and relying upon what the Bible said to be true. My shaky faith was the result of a person new to the things of Christ, who did not know God or his ways very well. If as believers we find ourselves stuck at the base camp of truth instead of ascending the heights of scriptural realities, we will struggle ever to enjoy God or navigate the Christian life well. This would be a great sadness, as if there is one thing that God does crave, it is that truth be known so that freedom may ensue.

An inconsistent parent?

Somewhat naively perhaps, little children expect their parents to be consistent. Their growth and maturity depend on many set routines. During the school term they arise from bed and eat meals at certain times. Grudgingly they even return to their beds according to the parental clock. If children step out of line, something unpleasant usually happens and so they come to order their worlds according to patterns that will enable the most comfortable journey possible through to adulthood.

Is God an inconsistent parent? A casual flicker through the Bible might have left you with this impression. He appears both angry and kind to people doing the same things. If this is really the case, then no wonder there is doubt concerning your standing with God. You're just watching the same programme but he keeps shifting from angry Dad to kind Dad!

Subjects like the wrath of God, hell and final judgment are met with awkward silence in the lives of many Christians today. Perhaps this is because in our post-modern world (whatever that means this week) with no absolutes and certainly no accountability to a deity, we think that talking about God's wrath or the subject of a coming judgment is, well, just not good PR for God! Additionally it makes us Christians look like extreme fanatics and after all, surely in our present day, God needs all the help he can get to rescue his ailing reputation!

Perhaps then we should simply maintain the awkward silence and ignore the nasty bits? Yet if we choose to do so, our understanding of God's kindness in grace will be severely limited. I believe that both the wrath and grace of God need bringing into plain view and with sharp focus. Indeed, the wonders of grace can only be appreciated in full measure once the wrath is also illuminated. You might wonder how these two can possibly fit together, but the latter is vitally important to understanding the former.

I wonder if a casual flicker through the Bible sometimes leaves you feeling rather confused? Anyone who has ever tried to read through it in one go will understand my point. I mean Genesis is absorbing and really exciting but by the time you get to Numbers, there is page after page of numbers. Why is this, what is the point? Leviticus can be equally bewildering with an ample supply of tassels on people's clothes and an alarming number of goats! The reality is that we need to understand the doctrine they illustrate in order to move truth from merely an intellectual puzzle to practical application. It can be exactly the same when we come to consider the wrath of God.

Perhaps a very spiritual person doesn't read the Bible in order, for he is 'led by the Spirit'. He says "Lord speak to me today. I pray that wherever I open the Bible and put my finger, then that will be your word for me today". So he does that and it lands at Ezekiel 25 v17: *'I will carry out great vengeance on them and punish them in my wrath. Then they will know that I am the Lord, when I take vengeance on them.'*

He exclaims: "Lord that was obviously the devil. I pray this time Lord that you will really speak to me." This time his finger lands at Ezekiel 24 v14: *'I the Lord have spoken. The time has come for me to act. I will not hold back; I will not have pity, nor will I relent. You will be judged according to your conduct and your actions, declares the Sovereign Lord.'* So now he thinks: "Lord, I'll have one more go, third time lucky (no I don't believe in that)". Ezekiel 27 v36 appears and says: *'You will come to a horrible end and will be no more'!*

He's not normally like that!

Many of us as Christians read things like these verses and feel somewhat apologetic for God. A new Christian comes to church and starts devouring scripture and then they approach you and say, "I've read this in Ezekiel" and you feel you want to say: 'Well he's not normally like that; I do apologise'.

I can remember when our son was growing up. Once he just lay down in a supermarket and screamed for all his worth, as they do. So you drag them along into some room and mumble in embarrassment, 'He's not normally like this, he's tired'! We feel like this with God. 'I'm ever so sorry, he got really angry there; he's not normally like that.'

It's here we need to understand our western atheistic culture that says there is no judgment; we are not accountable to God and there is no wrath. But the sobering fact is the Bible shows there is unrelenting, sustained anger and righteous wrath from God being poured out upon humanity in all generations. The scale of it is enormous. Just look at some of these things it says in Ezekiel: *'Great waves of unrelenting wrath'; 'I will not have pity'; 'I will not hold back'; 'I will not relent'; 'there is no mercy' and 'You will come to a horrible end and be no more'.* This is not God mildly irritated, this is a vengeful, wrathful, angry God who is forever just.

What should be more shocking to us is not that God gets angry, but that God did not kill you and me last night in our sleep because of the things we think and do and say. Our culture responds, 'We are not accountable to God and have done nothing to deserve wrath.' However, the commandments say: 'Love the Lord your God with all your heart, your mind, your soul and your strength.' On that alone we fail terribly. The creator God who made us for his glory and has the right to hold us accountable, has the right to be wrathful when we disobey him.

Maybe we think, well even if God is wrathful then grace means he has calmed down a bit. We suppose that obviously by the time the New Testament arrives, God has realised he set the bar too high. Perhaps the Ten Commandments should have been Ten Suggestions? Grace just becomes another word for tolerance. Perhaps we can get in our minds that somehow Jesus' death on the cross is God announcing the big let off. Maybe Jesus' death provided us with some kind of divine role model to aspire to. Another idea is that this lovely cuddly God now comes towards us, and as for the wrath of God, well he's so sorry about that, it was just so 'OT' of him! He's much more post-modern now and is not into that 'wrath' stuff anymore. Surely these ideas are not the answer. Scripture makes clear in Malachi 3:6, *'I the Lord do not change'.* There is no realignment of God's nature going on to suit the prevailing culture of the day.

Of Hell and the coming judgment

Colossians 3:6 says, speaking of the sinful principles by which the world operates, 'on account of these the wrath of God is coming'. The gospel is not that wrath no longer exists in the heart of God. The gospel is that a way of escape from the coming wrath has been made. We have a sure way of escape! Born out of his love God finds a way for his wrath to be satisfied but not abandoned. This is the victory summarised in James 2:13 where 'mercy triumphs over judgment'.

The caricature of odd people walking around with sandwich boards foretelling 'the end of the world drawing nigh' is not something I encourage, as it hinders people in our culture from considering a reasonable faith. However, we simply cannot reinterpret scripture to sanitize the bits showing God's wrath or the consequences of a life lived without reference to the Saviour. Neither can we avoid reference to them as of less importance than the bits about God's love and forgiveness. We need to be able to handle what we read, not rob it of meaning or change God's nature to something more domesticated. We must humbly accept God's self-disclosure of his character and nature through scripture as what it is: 'accurate disclosure' not 'conceptual theory'.

God gets angry at sin. God will judge sin and sinners. Hell is a real place, albeit somewhere no human was created to inhabit. God intends to assign the devil and his demons to this place. We are all facing hell without Christ; the reality is we all deserve it and the only way to escape it is to realise that and admit it, looking then for the one who can rescue us, as we realise we have no power to rescue ourselves. But make no mistake: hell is real, eternal and a place of isolation, of utter loneliness, despair, regret and selfishness; a vast and empty nothingness full of the pain that comes with facing that. It is truly a hopeless place of incompleteness as, although it is a place sustained by God, it is a place without any future salvation on offer. It's a place of our choosing. On the final day no-one will be able to point the finger at God and say he is being unfair and unjust. By nature God does all things well and all his actions and judgments are praiseworthy.

Psalm 145:17: *'The Lord is righteous in all his ways and kind in all his works.'*

Attempts have been made to reduce hell to more manageable parameters: not eternal, an absence of pleasure and not a presence of pain and distress. While it is true that we only get glimpses of its full horror, we still do receive descriptions through Scripture. We get more than enough to get the idea! Only as we embrace the fact we deserve hell can the gospel have any real meaning at all. We cannot of ourselves avoid it and need a saviour because there is something we need saving from.

Unpalatable truths in the Bible simply cannot be covered over to suit our culture. Take for example:

Psalm 137:7-10:

'Remember, O LORD, against the Edomites
* the day of Jerusalem,*
how they said, "Lay it bare, lay it bare,
* down to its foundations!"*
O daughter of Babylon, doomed to be destroyed,
* blessed shall he be who repays you*
* with what you have done to us!*
Blessed shall he be who takes your little ones
* and dashes them against the rock!'*

Admittedly the imagery and language used to describe the visitation of God's wrath upon this sinful culture seems extreme. At first glance the verses seem to suggest that God was pleased when Babylonian infants were killed. To help us understand what is being communicated we must remember that this passage is brimming with poetic language and metaphor designed to convey how deeply God feels about sin. Consideration of the issue at heart further reveals that this was a civilisation that prized and promoted the torture, abuse and suffering of others. What God actually wanted was to halt the ongoing perpetuation of such cruelty. This is conveyed in his expressed desire to see such evil come to an end and meant this culture having no future. In the same way we feel anger at suffering and injustice we can also see the heart of love in God within the heart of judgment if we understand the context.

It is appropriate to be angry when our newspapers and televisions report appalling treatment of people by others. Murder, abuse, cruelty and suffering to man or animal stir us with a just cry that this is not right and should not be happening. "Someone must pay for what they have done!" Our consciences are appalled. Imagine a whole nation and culture of people who lived in wholesale acts of this kind. Would we not demand and desire justice be done against such people? As part of our human nature is made in God's image, we still carry something of God's heart for justice and of his anger against injustice and pain. This is true even with the warping of sin in our lives. Why then do we find it hard to allow God to be portrayed in the full measure of his nature and character?

God is just and hates wickedness and evil and has promised there is a day coming. It has been appointed in heaven and each day brings us closer to that time when judgment will be apportioned. Someone may observe: "If this is true then how can I spend the rest of my life not cowering in the fear that I might actually be on the wrong side of this judgment when it comes?" Can a person be absolutely sure like the book of Hebrews encourages?

Hebrews 4:16: *'Let us then approach the throne of grace with confidence, so that we may receive mercy and find grace to help us in our time of need.'*

God is always angry at sin, he always will be angry at sin, he's never going to stop being angry at sin. He does not jump from wrath to love and then back again like some schizophrenic deity. God actually has a problem because his righteousness means his wrath has to be completely and justly satisfied. He can't just say, 'let's forget that and start again'. Amazingly we will see later that wrath and the grace of God are not opposites but that actually one brings out the beauty in the other. Like the brilliance of the sun after the darkest of thunderstorm clouds, wrath and grace work together to magnify the Lord's love and mercy and his absolute righteousness in all his dealings.

Are we really that bad?

Jesus said: "it's not what goes into a man that defiles him". It's not the flesh that feeds the heart, it's the heart that feeds the flesh, and so what comes out of a man's heart is what defiles him. Every human being from the moment of being conceived has a dirty, sinful, fallen nature. This automatically means once life begins it produces dirt: thoughts and acts of sinful behaviour that become visible on the outside. Now it is true that the amount of dirt on the outside can vary. In fact some people are better than others and not everyone is as bad as everybody else, otherwise we would all be killing each other! God in his mercy restrains evil.

However, it's the evil basis of what we are inside that makes our behaviour dirty to varying degrees. No matter how good we are, not one of us is completely clean. Some people see themselves as good when compared to others and indeed they might well be. They may be on a mountain top of righteous behaviour in life when compared to others all around who are in the figurative gutter of sin. However, whether on the mountain top or in the gutter, neither is able to touch the stars. God is holy completely and a clean, pure nature is essential to be reflective of God's nature and to enjoy fellowship with him.

For people who fail to grasp this, it seems that being loved and accepted by God is only possible by working to earn it. They must convince themselves they are worth loving and perhaps never seriously face their personal problems that lurk within and lurch out like vomit. They do not forgive others as a result and even unleash unrestrained anger and criticism at those who do not meet the perceived standards. They're often unable to receive any correction but are quite happy to give it.

Such people are incapable of stopping and being loved by God for who they are and not for what they do. If ever they did stop, it would be to crash and burn. They become increasingly calloused to other people's feelings as more and more they attempt to stave off the gnawing pressure of guilt, resentment and a growing sense of not quite knowing the God they profess to follow. How do they think God feels about them; what would he say if suddenly appeared before them? Are the promises of his love in Scripture really theirs? They have no experience of crying 'Abba Father' as for them it is all about pleasing a hard task master.

An impossible standard

The reality of our fallen condition and inability to save ourselves is illustrated well in both teaching and narrative. First, Jesus' teaching in Matthew 5:20 says: *'For I tell you, unless your righteousness exceeds that of the scribes and Pharisees, you will never enter the kingdom of heaven'.*

Second, in verse 48 he says: 'You therefore must be perfect, as your heavenly Father is perfect'. These two verses are hard enough but he then continues through specifics just to make the point irrefutable, as generalities when talking about sin might make us feel an absence of personal application. He comments in verses 21-48 on sins such as anger, lust, divorce, retaliation to wrongs and love for our enemies. Each example is a blow to self-righteous hearts. In each case he states the Law of Moses but then shows that outward conformity to such laws is unacceptable to God as an act of righteousness. Why? Because Jesus shows us that it is the heart that is dirty and out of that flows all the sin we then see on the outside.

Even if we have not outwardly sinned it is just as possible to sit and think about the sin. But Jesus says that even if in your heart you feel anger, lust or hatred, it is a sin even before you commit a wrong deed. There is nothing you can do about this and yet without being clean you cannot be saved from facing judgment for your sins before almighty God on that terrible day when he will judge the living and the dead.

God wanted to leave us in no doubt that perfection like his is the required standard. He points out as if to drive it home to any who might think they can match the call, that our righteousness must exceed the Pharisees, who in human terms reached lifestyles of external acts of righteousness way beyond most people. These two facts nail every proud notion of being able to justify ourselves before God. We are not perfect and even the standards we may reach will likely be exceeded by others who themselves cannot attain perfection. The Pharisees were professional and skilled at doing good things and even they are shown to fail. This 'double whammy' of hopelessness is Jesus' intention. By holding up the righteous requirements of the Law he holds up a mirror to us and it shocks us and drives us in search of a saviour with the cry 'who can help me?'

As Robert Murray McCheyne puts it: 'Clear conviction of sin is the only true origin of dependence on another's righteousness, and, therefore, (strange to say) of the Christian's peace of mind and cheerfulness'. [2]

True that when it dawns on each of us that we are sinners it causes more distress and feels more intolerable to some than to others. But it is common to all on their journey to finding Christ that when they look into their own souls they see nothing but 'an abyss of sin' and they realise they cannot find the resources of righteousness on their own to save themselves. This recognition is the only true root to finding genuine salvation and thereafter Christian joy and happiness.

'Run John run the law demands
But gives me neither feet nor hands
Better news the gospel brings
It bids me fly and gives me wings'

John Bunyan [3]

3 *The four cups*

One cup clean inside and out
In two, disease is rife
The third cup cleansed by Christ alone
The fourth, a pure life

At some point during the conversion process there comes a sovereign work of the Holy Spirit; an awakening within us to the realities of the gospel. We will all have different stories of how this 'awakening' took place; suddenly or slowly. It will however have the same features; a realisation that we have sinned before God and are guilty, for *'no-one is righteous not even one'* (Romans 3:10).

Awareness occurs of our responsibility to be holy in how we live combined with the realisation of a complete inability to do so. 'But I see in my members another law, making me captive to the law of sin that dwells within my members' (Romans 7:23). Scripture shows us more clearly where we have sinned, for 'through the law comes the knowledge of sin' (Romans 3:20). Knowledge of God's law through scripture also provokes sin in us: *'but sin seizing an opportunity through the commandment, produced in me all kinds of covetousness'* (Romans 7:8). The more we understand of what God requires the more our fallen nature provokes our flesh to sin and rebel against it. We are more wretched than we think!

Although we must be careful not to separate the humanity of man into bits too much, as we are integrated beings, the New Testament touches on a distinction between our flesh and nature in most of the Epistles. Additionally words like 'heart', 'soul' and 'spirit' are also used to describe our inner being and therefore we may be confused as to what the difference is. Some translations are more helpful in consistency than others in this and in addition some scriptures use these words interchangeably in other contexts.

Substantially speaking however, the aspects of flesh and nature are key components weaved into the 'fearful' and 'wonderfully made' creations we are and absolutely crucial to understanding salvation correctly. Paul saw the understanding of them as a key foundational issue for churches to grasp. He used illustrations and examples to convey the truths he was communicating. These are often blunt instruments when it comes to full detail, but the meaning can be clearly seen.

Let me emphasise how salvation works through an illustration using cups to achieve a similar end. I hope this will bring additional clarity as to what Jesus meant when speaking to the Pharisees about cleaning the inside and outside of the cup or bowl. In each case the inside of the cup refers to what the Bible calls our nature. It can either be the new nature received through being united to Christ or the sinful nature, sometimes called our 'old man' or 'old self'. For example, *'We know that our old self was crucified with him ....'* (Romans 6:6)

The outside of the cup refers to what the Bible calls our flesh; 'the life I now live in the flesh I live by faith in the Son of God (Galatians 2:20). Our flesh is not the same as our sinful nature. Rather it is the vehicle through which our nature (which is the governing disposition within us) expresses itself through thoughts, actions, appetites, emotions and bodily desires. We are unable to clearly distinguish a notable difference between 'nature' and 'flesh', as we simply feel, act, speak and think as human beings. However, we are given revelation through scriptures concerning our make up in this. This we accept by faith as we do other truths in scripture.

Cup one – clean inside and out

The first cup is completely clean both inside and out. When Adam was created he was clean on the inside and outside. He had a heart after God, he obeyed God, his acts and lifestyle were pleasing to God because his heart was motivated to do so. Jesus himself said 'it is not what goes into a man that makes him unclean but what comes out of the heart'. Adam walked and fellowshipped with God. God made him and all of creation 'very good'.

Comparing Adam to a perfectly clean cup raises an interesting question concerning the state of his being. If so perfect, how could the devil in the form of a serpent trick him into doing something that had such serious implications for mankind? If a person was goaded into stealing an apple from a market stall today then the penalty would surely be nothing more than a stiff reprimand! Yet it is safe to argue that only one other punishment so severe and so seemingly inappropriate has ever been meted out in the history of the world. Of course I am talking about the cross of Jesus.

What a mystery that Adam could be tempted to sin when in full occupation of a perfect body both inside and out. How could he fall when his very nature was pure and perfect? Only God can reveal this, but to help a little with this interesting and almost inevitable question, I start with a good friend who lives in Latvia. He sent me a video clip recently showing him driving his car on the ice of a lake frozen near to where he lives. He was confidently speeding across the wide expanse without any concern for falling through. Theology can be a bit like ice!

We have the thick and solid ice of clear revelation from Scripture. For instance, Jesus is fully God and fully human, both natures in the one person of Christ. We know this as the

Bible makes it abundantly clear. The ice is thick and providing we have confidence that the Scriptures are trustworthy and a plumbline for all that is true (which they are) then we could drive a truck on that ice with no fear of it cracking or being seen to have a flaw in it.

Mystery and revelation

On the other hand there are some things we can ask questions about which the Bible either does not comment on at all or only gives us enough to have our faith satisfied. Even this will only be so if we are able to handle it correctly and our curiosity may still remain. Simply put, there are some things that only God knows, things he has chosen not to reveal. This is his decision and we must accept that such mysteries do not require solving in order to fully know him and the salvation he offers through Christ. Daniel 2:22 says: *'He reveals deep and hidden things; he knows what is in the darkness.'* We rely on God to show us all things as he chooses.

Have you ever tried to imagine what God looks like? It's impossible, for he does not have 'parts' as we do; he exists without shape or form or dimension. As has been said, 'his centre is everywhere, his circumference nowhere' 4. He exists without reference to time or space and is eternally present at every point in all universes and throughout all time. He exists without any constraint and this is something beyond our ability to understand.

If I clenched my fist and asked you to guess what I was holding, you would know firstly there was something. Also that it was relatively small to be hidden in my clenched fist, and perhaps that it was not sharp or very hot or cold as I would not be able to hold it tightly. These limited pieces of revelation would be known by what was observed.

It is the same with knowing what God is like based on what we observe. He has created green grass, blue sky, trees and the like. We can tell something about God from these, even perhaps that he likes blue and green a lot! We can tell he is big, creative, very powerful and wise. These things we know from the general revelation of nature around us. The things God has made provoke all humanity in some measure to consider them and know something of the one who made them.

Of course, more is revealed to us through Christ himself and Scripture which, as Paul tells us in 2 Timothy 3:16, is 'breathed out by God and profitable for teaching, for reproof, for correction, and for training in righteousness'. However, we can only know more by receiving greater revelation. It requires that his hands be opened yet further upon his initiative for us to see things we otherwise could not know or find out through our limited human capacities. Interestingly, Paul says in Ephesians 3:8-9:

'Grace was given to me, to preach to the Gentiles the unsearchable riches of Christ and to bring to light for everyone what is the plan of the mystery hidden for ages in God who created all things…'

What this means is that through the passage of time, as scripture records the revelation of God to each successive generation from Adam to Christ, we find more and more being revealed of God's plans for man. These are things that were hidden from the beginning of time; they are things that prophets prophesied about but then longed to know exactly what their prophecies would look like. Isaiah, as he spoke out what we now call his 53rd chapter must have wondered what and who is this suffering servant, who will bear sin and be crushed by God.

Paul talks of the hidden mystery, now made known to us on whom the fulfilment of the age has come. He knew that what was hidden was an open secret for all men to come to know the Saviour. This gospel was entrusted to him to communicate to the gentile world as it was then. He could talk of it as God had revealed it through Christ on the Cross.

We are not just recipients of grace in the saving act as we place our trust in Christ for the forgiveness of sins. We are also recipients of grace in that God was pleased to make known to us the mystery of Christ. He opened his hand and revealed to us what was and would have remained hidden.

Might it happen again?

We find a very illuminating scripture in the first epistle of Peter: 1 Peter 1:18-20: '… *knowing that you were ransomed from the futile ways inherited from your forefathers, not with perishable things such as silver or gold, but with the precious blood of Christ, like that of a lamb without blemish or spot. He was foreknown before the foundation of the world but was made manifest in the last times for the sake of you.*'

This Scripture shows that in the counsel of heaven, God knew before the world or man was made that a saving act would be required and that his son was to be the vehicle for this. He purposed and decided beforehand the exact time and nature of this salvation act and when it would be required. This is the 'thick ice' of scriptural revelation. Whether it was inevitable Adam was to fall and quite how this relates then to human responsibility or (freewill) and the sovereignty of God is moving to 'thin ice' if we try to be too dogmatic. There are some issues where dogma is completely inappropriate. Clearly he had a sinless nature but somehow was 'liable to slip'.

Is it possible, then, that once we get to the fullness of God's Kingdom at the second coming of Christ that it might all go wrong again? The earth and heavens are renewed, and sin, Satan, pain and death have been thrown into the lake of fire and destroyed completely, yet the liability to slip still remains. How can we be assured that man will not fall again and require yet more salvation? After all he was perfect once and fell so he might just do it again.

To answer this concern we must reckon on the clear fact that Christ was set apart before the foundation of the world to save mankind. Before his crucifixion he had not made atonement and until the fall it was not required. Now that he has made atonement, he has died and been raised once for all. Perhaps, his raised and resurrected body will even bear the scars and marks of the suffering endured for all eternity. On this, Scripture is unclear, but as to what has been achieved, let us look at what the writer to the Hebrews observed:

Hebrews 9:24-28: *'For Christ has entered, not into holy places made with hands, which are copies of the true things, but into heaven itself, now to appear in the presence of God on our behalf. Nor was it to offer himself repeatedly, as the high priest enters the holy places every year with blood not his own, for then he would have had to suffer repeatedly since the foundation of the world. But as it is, he has appeared once for all at the end of the ages to put away sin by the sacrifice of himself. And just as it is appointed for man to die once, and after that comes judgment, so Christ, having been offered once to bear the sins of many, will appear a second time, not to deal with sin but to save those who are eagerly waiting for him.'*

The enormity of the historical event of the cross from an eternal perspective cannot be underestimated. Christ died once, for all. This act is so powerful and final that it precludes any potential need for any other saving act through all out the ages of eternity to come. So full and final is it that our eternal state and destiny has been fully secured by it and we have been told that this is the case.

Why Adam fell lies alongside other questions such as 'where did evil come from?' and 'how and why did Satan fall?' We must leave by faith these thin ice questions, where revelation but not truth is limited to our view, in the hands of him who has revealed all we need for life and salvation. Somehow our restored nature in Christ is more secure than Adam's ever was and not by our own efforts but by the enormity of the work of the Cross. We are in Christ; the same power that raised Christ from the dead is now at work in us.

Cup two – dirty all over

With the second cup we see that somehow Adam's pure and sincere heart for God gave in when tempted by Satan. The deceiver tried many years later also to tempt Jesus but praise God that Jesus withstood. Adam however did not and by choosing to disobey God he and all humanity ended up with a fallen nature.

What was clean and pure essentially in nature on the inside became corrupted and dirty. What is on the inside will eventually be displayed through acts on the outside. Over the first few chapters of Genesis we see humanity gradually becoming more and more dirty on the outside, perhaps most notably with Cain and Abel in Genesis 4:3-7:

'In the course of time Cain brought to the LORD an offering of the fruit of the ground, and Abel also brought of the firstborn of his flock and of their fat portions. And the LORD had regard for Abel and his offering, but for Cain and his offering he had no regard. So Cain was very angry, and his face fell. The LORD said to Cain, "Why are you angry, and why has your face fallen? If you do well, will you not be accepted? And if you do not do well, sin is crouching at the door. Its desire is for you, but you must rule over it.'

Cain found anger and resentment in his heart which ultimately led him to murder his brother. God told him that the sin at the door of his heart must be mastered, but this he was unable to do. The fall of man told in Genesis 3 had rendered all human hearts spiritually dead, unable to bring themselves to life and into relationship with God. Sin has separated us from the life of God. All of us are 'dead in sin', as told in Ephesians 2.

With a sinful nature come acts of the flesh that are sinful. Because our essential nature is dirty the flesh becomes dirty. The Bible catalogues the kind of behaviour that developed, 'Now the works of the flesh are evident: sexual immorality, impurity, sensuality, idolatry, sorcery, enmity, strife, jealousy, fits of anger, rivalries, dissensions, divisions' (Galatians 5:19). So much so, that by the time of Noah it could not have got much blacker. We read 'every inclination of man's heart all the time was evil'. In this context more and more evil was then manifested outwardly so God wiped mankind out, all except for Noah and his family who he found alone to be righteous and walking with God in his generation.

What a contrast we have from the story of Cain in Genesis to the account of Jesus in Matthew 4:

'Then Jesus was led up by the Spirit into the wilderness to be tempted by the devil. And after fasting forty days and forty nights, he was hungry. And the tempter came and said to him, "If you are the Son of God, command these stones to become loaves of bread." But he answered, "It is written, 'Man shall not live by bread alone, but by every word that comes from the mouth of God.'

Then the devil took him to the holy city and set him on the pinnacle of the temple and said to him, "If you are the Son of God, throw yourself down, for it is written, 'He will command his angels concerning you,' and 'On their hands they will bear you up, lest you strike your foot against a stone.'[7] Jesus said to him, "Again it is written, 'You shall not put the Lord your God to the test.'

Again, the devil took him to a very high mountain and showed him all the kingdoms of the world and their glory. And he said to him, "All these I will give you, if you will fall down and worship me." Then Jesus said to him, "Be gone, Satan! For it is written, 'You shall worship the Lord your God and him only shall you serve.' Then the devil left him, and behold, angels came and were ministering to him.'

Here we see Christ tempted in a variety of ways over a sustained period of time. Unlike Cain, and also unlike any of Adam's descendants, Christ resisted at every turn and overcame temptation. Sometimes it has been said 'It was easier for Christ to resist sin than for us as he was God'. Another way of looking at it, though, is that he has been tempted to a level most men never get to as we usually find our flesh giving in to the areas we are weakest in, so most of us do not know just how powerful and agonising the full power of temptation resisted can be for a human being. Christ could say to us 'you might say I do not know what you go through. I would say to you that you do not know what I had to go through and still won'.

Christ showed, to continue our analogy, the 'clean inside' of the cup, a nature fully obedient to God and sinless in every way. We however cannot defeat sin and master it as from birth we have a cup which is 'dirty on the inside' and unable through our effort to be cleaned. We need a miracle, a new nature and not self-improvement. We are also responsible for change. 'You must master it' was God's observation to Cain, yet he was not able to do so. God would say to us 'you must master it' but we also find we are not able. Realising our responsibility for change and our actions yet also our utter impotence in being able to do anything about it is a pre-requisite to anyone coming to know the Lord. It is why Paul, illustrating the spiritual journey of someone coming to know the Lord, in Romans 7:21-25 says:

'So I find it to be a law that when I want to do right, evil lies close at hand. For I delight in the law of God, in my inner being, but I see in my members another law waging war against the law of my mind and making me captive to the law of sin that dwells in my members. Wretched man that I am! Who will deliver me from this body of death? Thanks be to God through Jesus Christ our Lord!'

Cup three – clean on the inside

It is against this backdrop of failure that the Holy Spirit brings us to see our continuing incapability of keeping the righteous requirements of God. So in desperation for a solution we find Christ's righteousness is offered as a free gift, not only sufficient for dealing with our sin but also able to do something about the immobility of our dead hearts.

On acceptance, the cup 'dirty on the inside' is decisively changed into a third cup that is clean on the inside. The new believer finds he is no longer identified in and with Adam but in and with Christ. Sin no longer has mastery as 2 Corinthians 5:17-18 proclaims:

'Therefore, if anyone is in Christ, he is a new creation. The old has passed away; behold, the new has come. All this is from God, who through Christ reconciled us to himself.'

Being 'born again' means becoming 'clean on the inside'. This is not a feeling or some kind of enabling that allows a person to make himself clean and adjust his nature. Rather it is a fact promised by Scripture that sees a total identity change take place to the essential nature of a person. It is completed by Christ's power being sufficient to do it without any help or aid from me and at no cost to me. It is applied by the Holy Spirit purely by my receiving this gift through faith trusting that Christ's sinless life and obedient death before God on my behalf is sufficient to cleanse and change me.

Christ has done all that is required through his obedient life and his atoning sacrifice to make provision for me and to be acceptable before God as regards my sin. Once a person has accepted by faith this work of Christ, trusting it to be enough for them and believing it is effective for them, then the sin accumulated in the life of such a person is no longer an obstruction.

Cup four – clean inside and out

Where the dirt of a fallen nature increasingly corrupts the flesh in our illustration of the second cup, the fourth cup also produces change on the outside. A new nature born of God naturally begins to clean our flesh, our thoughts, appetites, emotions and bodily desires.

Ephesians 4 refers to *'until we all reach maturity'.* This ongoing journey towards knowing Christ more fully in our hearts and being like Christ more in the outworking of our lives is a journey we will always be on until he returns.

The hope of the Christian is not of dying and going to heaven and somehow existing in a disembodied state. Neither is the idea of heaven as a place of singing endless worship songs accurate. Both of these distorted hopes create the image of a totally foreign environment and lifestyle, misinterpreting what it means to be human, living in relationship with God and created in his image. That caricature of the future owes more to Gnosticism, which was a huge influence of error challenging the early church, than it does to the Bible. Paul encountered the emergence of Gnostic thinking and brought correction to its claims, namely that our bodies of flesh and bones - and in fact anything material - was inherently evil and an encumbrance which one day we would be rid of.

Whilst it is true that if we die before Christ comes, our bodies are left on earth and decay, we only find ourselves **temporarily** 'away from the body and at home with the Lord'. When Christ returns 1 Corinthians tells us we will be clothed with immortality and our bodies will be raised incorruptible. We will again have our bodies back raised from the dead. Earth will be liberated from its bondage to decay. It will not be killed off and removed but rather be released and birthed. Somehow heaven and earth will merge.

Let's cast our minds to the future when all things are made new and we have the perfect bodies we are destined to receive and enjoy, in perfect fellowship with God. We are told that unlike Adam our bodies will be secure in their perfected state for all time. The new creation will not fall again, not commence another cycle of sin under the groaning weight of natural disasters that devastate us now.

The crucifixion of Jesus is a 'once and for all' sacrifice and when all things are made new, 'death itself will be thrown into the lake of fire'. We will be like Cup One; clean on the inside and clean on the outside but not liable to fall to this terrible fate again. Our flesh will be fully redeemed and we will enjoy fellowship with God in a renewed heaven and earth, walking with him, incorruptible. All that was originally made good by God will be good again, even better than before. The glory of the Saviour will shine. The nature and character of God will be displayed to a redeemed humanity looking on and enjoying his works for all eternity. Never again will we suffer a downward pull of nature and never again have to say 'no' to the flesh. We shall be like Christ and we shall see him as he is. What was lost and marred in Genesis will be lived out now in restored completeness forevermore.

However until that time comes, we as Christians live in a process of being made holy, already experiencing redemption of the flesh to some degree. The cup that has been instantly cleansed on the inside starts to become gradually cleaner on the outside, although it will never become perfectly clean until our bodies are 'raised incorruptible'. The amount of cleansing that occurs depends on what we do with the gift of salvation.

So where do I stand with God?

The illustration of four cups places Christians at various points between the third and fourth cups as we press on to becoming more like Christ. In later chapters we will look at how God helps us on our journey, through the provision and outworking of grace in different areas. Before this can be done, however, do we grasp fully the meaning of grace? Grace is essentially the kindness of God revealed in acts of mercy and provision to those who do not deserve it. Without grace there would be no Christians! Grace is best illuminated when set within the context of wrath – God's righteous anger at the wickedness of mankind.

4 *Wrath and grace*

Feast your eyes
On the mighty tree
So majestic to behold
But remember the roots
In the depths beneath
For full glory to be told!

Like a diamond upon black cloth, it should come as no surprise that the grace of God shines more brightly when displayed against the wrath of God at the wretchedness of humanity. A correct understanding of this is going to be very important for the future of the church. In our efforts to display the diamond in culturally relevant ways within areas such as humanistic Europe, the black background must not be removed. If we do so, the gospel will be robbed of its fullness. We will see and celebrate Jesus' death as defeating sin and death on behalf of mankind but fail to see that the wrath of God was ours to face personally. It had to be and was removed by Christ, a most amazing rescue mission indeed. So let me pull this most precious of diamonds out from beneath the counter for a closer look.

Titus 3 v 4 says: *'But when the kindness and love of God our Saviour appeared, he saved us.'*

This verse doesn't refer to a time when God started being kind and loving. God has always been kind and loving, but it was at this time when his kindness and love were revealed. Paul talks about the mystery, hidden for ages, now being displayed. The verse continues: 'When the kindness and love of God appeared, he saved us, not because of the righteous things we had done, but because of his mercy.'

God reveals this most amazing diamond of mercy for us to receive. In Romans 5 v 8-9 we read:

'God demonstrates his own love for us in this: While we were still sinners, Christ died for us. Since we have now been justified by his blood, how much more shall we be saved from God's wrath through him!'

If Paul had grace and wrath in the same verse in his gospel then our authentic gospel must also follow suit.

So how do we let the diamond sparkle in our lives? Imagine yourself for a while standing before God and it won't take long before uncomfortable feelings of extreme guilt emerge. Any feelings of confidence quickly slip away upon the realisation that you deserve neither pity nor mercy. You quite rightly surmise that you should 'come to a horrible end' to quote our verse from Ezekiel and incur the wrath of God. It is at this point that the good news of the gospel comes into view. Like a huge wave God's anger is looming upon you. But just before impact, it turns direction and crashes upon Jesus. The theological description for this would be propitiation through substitution!

Propitiation

Propitiation is a way or means of turning away the wrath of God. In this context a person, namely Jesus is the one who turns away this wrath.

Hebrews 2:16-18 explains: *'For surely it is not angels that he helps, but he helps the offspring of Abraham. Therefore he had to be made like his brothers in every respect, so that he might become a merciful and faithful high priest in the service of God, to make propitiation for the sins of the people. For because he himself has suffered when tempted, he is able to help those who are being tempted.'*

Jesus had to be like us in every way (human) so he could stand in our place. Yet he also had to be unlike us (God) as only God is without sin. Only in this way is there no punishment due to Christ for his own actions, thus allowing him to take ours and draw to himself the punishment due to us. He became our substitute and took full responsibility before God the Father for our sin.

2 Corinthians 5:21: *'For our sake he made him to be sin who knew no sin, so that in him we might become the righteousness of God.'*

In other words ownership of our sin was fully and totally transferred onto Christ so he bore in full that which was rightly ours to bear.

This does not mean God's anger has turned away, that it just petered out and stopped. Jesus was not sent to die so that God's anger would merely subside. Everything that God could ever have poured out on us in wrath, he poured out on Jesus instead. God did not cease to feel wrath by in some way Jesus doing enough to appease him. That would not be justice. No, the wrath of God at our sin was poured out fully onto Christ in the same way it would have been onto us.

Isaiah 63:2-4: *'Why is your apparel red, and your garments like his who treads in the winepress?' I have trodden the winepress alone, and from the peoples no one was with me; I trod them in my anger and trampled them in my wrath; their lifeblood spattered on my garments, and stained all my apparel. For the day of vengeance was in my heart, and my year of redemption had come.'*

In the above verses the prophet, somewhat perplexed, wonders why God's appearance is red like someone who has been working in a winepress. The answer that follows gives the prophet an insight that vengeance and judgment are costly and require the shedding of blood. There can be no justice without due punishment being received by those to whom it is due. Christ is the one who saves through his sacrifice, but equally is the one who judges righteously and punishes sin. We cannot have one aspect of who God is without the other as to do this would distort his purity and righteousness.

Let me give another illustration. Imagine the wrath of God as like a towel soaking in a bowl of water that represents his righteous anger towards our sin. As we are about to stand beneath the full towel, dripping with water, God squeezes out all his righteous anger fully and completely on another. Every last drop has gone: the towel is wrung completely dry. Punishment and judgment for every thought, deed and word that deserves God's wrath has been completely wrung out on Jesus. Every last drop of wrath has gone leaving nothing left to come. Once we are in Christ this incredible sacrifice becomes applied to our account so God will never again have an angry thought of judgment against you or I; it was all spent, wrung out with not even a drip left.

Isaiah 12 v 1: expresses it like this: *'I will praise you, O Lord. Although you were angry with me, your anger has turned away and you have comforted me.'*

Not only is anger spent on another, leaving us free, but we receive favour, protection and comfort instead. The active, ongoing predisposition of God towards us is now fixed for eternity as there is no longer anything to punish. Furthermore, in Psalm 138:7 we read: 'You stretch out your hand against the wrath of my enemies'. In addition to our liberation, we are also kept safe by his active protection over our lives from the evil plans and schemes of the Devil and his hosts of darkness.

While it is true that we do not face God's judgment any longer as Christians, we do face his discipline as our Father. His motivation is maturity not judgment. We can behave in ways he is stirred to correct because he loves us. Having begun a good work in us his desire is to complete it.

A finished work

When you come home from a long day at work, you sit down because your labour is finished. Christ also once ascended back to heaven, sat down at the right hand of God. He had completed his work: his last words were 'it is finished'! 'After making purification for sins, he sat down at the right hand of the majesty on high' (Hebrews 1:3) This meant everything required for the securing of salvation, the defeat and rendering powerless of the old sinful nature and the creation of a new nature in the life of a believer by the Holy Spirit. It meant a cup with a clean inside. All that is required is accomplished in full with no need for extra work to be done by him, or me, or anyone else to gain it or keep it. He sat down! He has completed the task with nothing left to accomplish. We now live the other side of a finished work.

Once 'in Christ' the believer is now and for all time changed. All sin past present and future is forgiven, nothing can change this transaction. Christ has also done all required, not only to present us clean and faultless before God, but also now as people able to be used by God. I can be given tasks and have callings planned by God himself! We all can. As we abide in Christ and he abides in us, so the promise of much fruit is ahead. There's no need to do extra things to qualify for usefulness. We need only to train the flesh to be more sharp in readiness and fervency for serving Christ and to live our God-given life enjoying growing intimacy and deepening fellowship with him.

Transaction complete

When propitiation has truly taken place, the Bible says, we can come boldly before the throne of grace. This is because God will never ever have an angry thought of judgment towards me or you again. Every thought of that kind has already been had and directed towards Jesus, our sin bearer.

Leviticus 16 speaks of the Day of Atonement where two goats were selected for offering. Clearly two goats are not enough to cleanse sin from people and as with all the sacrificial system of the Old Testament, it was merely a shadow or picture of what was to come in Christ as our great offering.

The first goat was killed and its blood shed; the second one was called the 'scapegoat'. The priest would lay his hands on the goat and confess the sins of the people, thereby transferring sins to the goat. It was then sent away into the wilderness taking with it the sin of the people. This is similar to that done by Jesus for us. John 1:29 says: 'Behold the lamb of God who takes away the sin of the world' while Isaiah 53:6 states: 'The Lord laid on him the iniquity of us all'. This taking away and turning wrath from us is captured in these pictures pre-figuring Christ.

With the wrath poured out on our scapegoat there is nothing left for him to be angry about. Even when I have a bad day and sin, God is not angry with me so that I must stand again before his judgment, because all anger has been squeezed out on Jesus. As this truth flows freely into my heart, chains of uncertainty about my standing before God, fall off. Those constant nagging doubts as to how he feels about me no longer have any room to take root and grow; there is no argument against a completed work like this on my behalf.

You may have had the most disgusting past possible, the most wretched existence that you dare not even confess to another human being. But once you understand from your head to your heart that everything you know you deserve was placed on Jesus, who can accuse you of anything? Every mouth is silenced, every accusing finger, stopped. This is why it is so important we preach the wrath of God. He who has been forgiven much, loves much. Isn't that amazing?

There is another powerful illustration which is important to get hold of. Not only did Jesus draw away the wrath of God, but the Apostle Paul adds:

Galatians 2:20: *'I have been **crucified with Christ** and I no longer live, but **Christ** lives in me. The life I live in the body, I live by faith in the Son of God, who loved me and gave himself for me.'*

Jesus did not just die to forgive my sins. He died in order that sin might die in me. I am not just forgiven, I am changed! Jesus was a second 'Adam' who made right what the first Adam ruined. Jesus is now called the firstborn amongst many brothers. A new humanity, a new people on the earth are emerging through and from his redeeming work. These are children not born from human decision or natural biological process as with children of the first Adam, these children are born from heaven, born of God. They are new creations and without condemnation.

God could have just forgiven and left me at an inferior level, but in fact he has also changed me by giving an impartation of his life to mine. I am joined with Christ for there is something of God that lives within me now. He has taken up residence in my life permanently. The law of sin which made me continually follow through a desire to sin against God, thus incurring his wrath, has now been changed. With my new nature, I actually don't want to sin anymore; it has become unattractive to me.

You may complain, 'Well why do I still have bad thoughts then?' The truth is that we continue to battle 'fleshly' desires; strong appetites, demands and opinions. Until Jesus comes again and our bodies are redeemed and catch up with our new nature, we will battle against 'the flesh'. We have to learn to reprimand it by saying 'I'm sorry, I'm not doing that, I don't want to'. The difference is like that of the trajectory between a stone and a sparrow in the air.

If I drop a stone, it will fall and hit the ground. As it contains no life, there is nothing to defy and fly against the law of gravity. It's dead and cannot resist. If I drop a sparrow it might fall for a little while but soon it will start to defy the pull of that which the stone could not resist. Similarly the life of God is within us now and we can defy the downward pull of sin and fly! We need to understand how radical the cross has been in its effects upon us. These are not always felt consciously to start with, but through the work of Christ, can be trusted as reliable facts. God assures us of their truth and therefore a confident stand can be made against our minds when feeling condemned.

It is essential therefore to orientate our thoughts and feelings around the truth revealed and not feelings perceived. The giving of our lives to Christ, perhaps by some simple prayer in faith expressed to God, does not always mean we will feel 'alive in Christ'. This is even though the gospel has been received and the Saviour's work for us understood. Such feelings are anticipated in Romans 6:6 where encouragement is given to reckon new life to be true because of what the Bible declares. The famous illustration of the time-zone change is helpful. My watch might say 3pm, but if I just have flown from the UK to Holland, it is in fact later whether I feel it or not. Once in Christ, we are in a new country and what he says is true, regardless of our feelings!

Bold approach

As the deep gaze into the diamond of the grace of God continues, the wrath magnifies the grace even more. As God's wrath has been satisfied he is now able to take up habitation with what was unclean. He is able to look at me as a holy temple where he lovingly and gladly dwells. The Bible says that the same power that raised Jesus from the dead is now at work in me.

Someone once said to me about Christians, 'people do not change'. This sad scepticism was born out of observation that many had not changed in ways that they should or could have. This does not mean, though, that change was not possible. If the power that raised a dead corpse to life is at work in me, surely any change that God desires is possible. We can and should be encouraged that whatever our previous behaviour and thought patterns, they can be changed through what the radical conversion to Christ brings.

That is also why we should expect people to be healed, set free and saved as we speak and act in the name of Jesus. We can demonstrate his kingdom because the same power is at work in us on his behalf. Peter and John said 'I haven't got anything of myself, but what I do have I give you'. How did they know what they had? It had moved from head to heart and anything then was possible. The truth set them free to live, act and think in accordance with God's will.

We are ambassadors of Christ, the presence of God continually with us whether it's a good or bad day. We can do the works that Jesus did any and every day on the basis of his new life is in us and we being new creations. It is the same power that raised Jesus from the dead that works in our bodies and lives. Churches need to be filled with people who think like this.

However, this truth is dangerous, almost to the point where we say: 'well, why don't we carry on sinning then?' If that thought pops up now and then because of the 'logical' argument, then you've understood the gospel. This vital and radical understanding of the gospel is important and seems to indicate we can be used by God without giving any regard to lifestyle, whether sinning or not.

So, we are 'right' in the sight of God all the time once we have accepted Christ. Regardless of our conduct or current behaviour the truth of our justification remains. This is a potentially scandalous and highly dangerous truth. Some people distorted this even in Paul's day by saying, 'Well therefore we can carry on sinning as this just makes God look all the more forgiving by giving him more to forgive!' Clearly this is not the point. New life creates in us a desire to please God from our very core. If genuinely saved, we are changed people.

5 *Working it out*

I'm loved – and the knowledge is pure energy!
I was wrestling with futility
Listening to conflicting tunes.
Now the fight is over,
I'm delighting in music
Where every note has purpose

Jesus was pure in both thought and deed. He was the second Adam, with a pure heart towards God and a faultless life displayed. 'Can any of you prove me guilty of sin?' he asked of the people in John 8:6. Jesus loved to serve his Father, he always obeyed, and he enjoyed the fellowship Adam once knew. Even when tempted by Satan as the first Adam was, Jesus withstood. As a man, he was tempted in every way as we are. As God, he alone won through for us.

Jesus died on the cross in our place, the righteous for the unrighteous. He had no sin of his own, either through nature or action, to bear. Instead, he took on our sin **and** responsibility for it before God. In doing this he broke the cycle of sin in fallen humanity. In exchange for taking our sin, Christ offered those of us who accept him as saviour, new life. His resurrection life and his purity, credited to us.

A radical miraculous change of the heart takes place through the miracle of this new birth. Jesus told Nicodemus that 'you must be born again'. We are brought to life by the Spirit of God. By faith in Christ our old nature has been crucified with him and replaced with a new nature. We do not feel this happen, although we should enjoy the effects of it through the joy of sins forgiven and old patterns of thought and behaviour being changed. This is a once-for-all event and results in a new nature that is totally, perfectly clean forever. How wonderful this message of grace!

Death to the dirty heart!

Some believers, however, particularly new Christians, face difficult challenges as they still find themselves sinning in the same ways they did before coming to Christ. At this point awareness of the difference of the nature and the flesh is vital. The extent to which you are still dirty on the outside is irrelevant to the change in the essential nature you now have through faith in Christ. The road to change is not easy, automatic or ever fully completed in this life. But it must be attended to. Progress is promised.

Paul spoke in Romans 12 of a transformation coming through the renewing of our minds. This encouragement means that over time it's possible to become a changed person in habits, actions, thoughts and words. In 2 Corinthians 3:18 he says *'We are being transformed from one degree of glory to another',* implying that we are becoming ever more like Jesus himself. This is as we embrace his discipline of change in our lives, seeking him and the aspects of his mission that we are personally called to.

The verse is not talking about our nature but our flesh which has to be trained in righteousness. It needs to catch up with the fact that we are now 'clean in nature'. This is why a Christian can have a pure heart and still do bad things. Our flesh, emotions, appetites and desires flow from unredeemed bodies and minds which until Christ returns are not going to be made completely pure and holy. We are in bondage to decay in our flesh, yet being renewed in new creation in our essential nature. We live in a tension of 'who we are, but who we are not yet able to be fully'.

Furthermore, all kinds of habits and dysfunctional behaviour are often brought into new Christian lives. Some people at the beginning, lack the maturity to process or begin to remedy all their outward sinful behaviour and thinking at once. It's therefore perfectly possible for people who are not Christians to appear more righteous. They may have been brought up within a moral framework and enjoyed a stable home with high ideals. In this way, they could easily outshine a new convert to Christ, who still has poor habits and patterns of behaviour/thoughts to address.

Nevertheless, inside anyone who has not come to saving faith in Christ, is a heart that stinks because it has not yet been made anew! This is what Ezekiel saw when he described a prophetic picture of God removing a heart of stone and giving instead a heart of flesh. He was illustrating the need for replacement of the old nature that is dead to God it with a new nature alive to Him. A stone heart is dead and unable to respond. A heart of flesh by contrast has life breathed into it. We are told in Ephesians 'you were dead' but God 'made you alive in Christ'. The very thing Ezekiel saw prophetically, has now come into the human arena. God has come in Christ and offers a new heart, a nature transformed by the miracle of new birth.

Persistent sinning

Paul tells us to put off the old way of living and evidence of this is what should normally be seen within church. However it sometimes happens that when people become Christians they take a while to clean up the outside of the cup, even though they have been made holy in nature in an instant. Perhaps they've lived a whole life of being abused, rejected and badly treated. Their backgrounds may be steeped in a particular habitual sin. They come to Christ, their sins are removed and their heart is cleansed. They are given a new heart and are justified before God by Christ's sacrifice, a free gift whereby he received what they deserve. This is momentous thinking. Is it any wonder it takes time to sink in?

On conversion, does thinking and programming change automatically? When people have been hurt by or have suffered abuse throughout life, can't we understand that for a time, they may be a walking nightmare within the church and remain notorious in the wider community. They may say and do wrong things, hurt people and feel hurt. They do all this as the flesh is conditioned to behaviour patterns brought about by a sinful lifestyle and personality. Yet they are still completely changed and clean on the inside because of receiving the gift of grace by faith in Christ.

Of course, at some point change will occur. In Matthew 7:20 Jesus told his disciples to recognise where people stood by the fruit they produced. Earlier in Matthew 3:7 John the Baptist warned the Pharisees and Sadducees to 'bear fruit in keeping with repentance'. True repentance produces change. It may take longer than normal but eventually it will occur. A positive sign of new life breaking through this is the person's own desire to change. Do they react to failure with abhorrence or do they accept it as normal living? Part and parcel of receiving a new nature is a love for Christ that does not sit happily with tolerating sin. In the same way that we get angry at those who offend our loved ones, so does our new nature revolt at the offence of sin.

Receiving new life is like moving to live in another country. If you are British you will be used to certain ways of behaving, such as standing in queues and sunbathing under clouds! Debating the great issues of life such as dog pedigrees, weather patterns and government affairs will be quite normal. After emigrating, however, you may be amongst people who have no idea you are angry at their pushing ahead of you onto the bus. Neither do they care to discuss the prospect of rain for the weekend as they have grown up in a different culture.

On becoming Christians we are part of a new nation or tribe. We are, as Peter says in his first letter, 'a holy nation, a people belonging to God'. This nation is made up of every tongue, tribe and nation. All people groups will be included in this new nation of 'one new man in Christ' that is the bride who Christ is returning for. Our lives now are caught up with acclimatising to a new country and culture as we take our place as citizens with a new identity in Christ.

'Brain washing' is required in the correct sense of the phrase. Paul is not saying, to use our cup analogy, 'clean up the inside'. We cannot do that as Jesus has already done it. Paul is saying 'clean up the outside'! Some believers can get this wrong as they think to themselves that if they sin: 'my old nature still seems the same' or 'I've not got a new nature'. To live thinking: 'I'm not clean on the inside' and therefore God has not pronounced cleanness upon me, will never produce either enjoyment of who we are in Christ or a lifestyle that reflects our new identity in him. We will forever be trying to climb the wrong hill.

Gradually the new nature will do what Paul says in Ephesians 4:22, that now you've come to know Christ, you are no longer to live like you have been used to living. Instead put off your old self that belongs to your former manner of life with its corrupt and deceitful desires. Be renewed in the spirit of your minds and put on the new self. Clean yourself up, get your flesh into line with your new holy and righteous nature for you are a new creation created after the likeness of God in true righteousness and holiness.

Demonisation

Amongst those who are genuinely saved and have a heart to please God, we find some who trip up over the same things again and again. It is not that they don't want to grow in the faith or live a life worthy of their calling. Indeed many wrong habits, thoughts, emotions, ways of talking or reacting may have been conquered. Yet certain things just won't yield and these people are left full of self-loathing and shame, wondering: 'How can God still love me when I just keep on doing this?'

Desperation to change coupled with a seeming powerless ability to do so may be caused by 'demonisation'. The Bible does not use the word 'possession' and it is important to note that a Christian cannot be 'possessed of the Devil' as this would signify ownership. However, a Christian can fall victim to demonisation ,which is the influence of demons, to a lesser or greater extent, on someone's life.

In the context of the need to avoid repetitive and deliberate sinful behaviour, Paul exhorts us in Ephesians 4, *'not to give the devil a foothold'.* This is to avoid opening up our lives to some degree of demonic power which will control our behaviour in certain things. If this happens, praying with trusted and wise, mature believers can be a source of freedom if change is truly desired. Roots of sin can be identified by the Holy Spirit and prayers of repentance and release spoken into the willing heart.

Do 'experienced' Christians get it wrong?

Some time ago a routine day of fasting and prayer came round that I had put in my diary. I have tried to set some kind of pattern for these things as otherwise they tend to drift. I made plans to eat an evening meal and then nothing more until the next evening meal. However during the evening my mind and stomach developed more and more of a captivation with the prospect of cheese and biscuits as an evening snack!

I tried to persuade myself to stick to the diary plan; but then thoughts of not being a legalist attacked, especially as this fast day was not a prompting of the Lord but a random diary date. Surely it could be better placed somewhere else to be more effective! Back and forth I paced, wrestling with my dilemma. A hard day had passed and a busy one lay ahead the next day, so time for prayer would be squeezed anyway.... Finally, I reasoned myself into a nice plateful of blue stilton and crackers with a resolution to reschedule fasting to a day more suitable when time was not so pressed.

Next morning, I had some time to walk and pray on the beach, as is often my habit. But as I started out, my weak flesh became a taunt. 'How can you think you are a man of prayer?', 'You cared more for your stomach than for the things you were going to pray for'. On and on it went so that I felt quite useless in prayer and a bit of a fraud. I believe God used my weakness of flesh to teach me something quite important. Two stories from Scripture were brought to my attention.

2 Kings 13:15-17: *'Elisha said to him, "Take a bow and arrows." So he took a bow and arrows. Then he said to the king of Israel, "Draw the bow," and he drew it. And Elisha laid his hands on the king's hands. And he said, "Open the window eastward," and he opened it. Then Elisha said, "Shoot," and he shot. And he said, "The LORD's arrow of victory, the arrow of victory over Syria! For you shall fight the Syrians in Aphek until you have made an end of them."*

In this account Elisha placed his hands on King Joab's hands, thus adding his anointing and the blessing of God upon Joab's own frailty. This was an act of undeserved grace and brought blessing and victory to the king whose weakness would have otherwise brought him to failure. In this case the nation had been growing weak through successive failure of God's appointed leaders to lead in his ways and his strength. Leaders had become weak and Joab realised he had too. He was then moved by his failure and impotence honestly to draw near to God for his enabling. God helps the obedient yet weak person who puts his hand on the bow. God will put his hand over ours and give us the strength we did not have. Then we fight the battle in the strength of God's faithfulness, not from the reservoir of our own strength.

Consider Jacob and Esau in Genesis 27:14-23:

'So he went and took them and brought them to his mother, and his mother prepared delicious food, such as his father loved. Then Rebekah took the best garments of Esau her older son, which were with her in the house, and put them on Jacob her younger son. And the skins of the young goats she put on his hands and on the smooth part of his neck. And she put the delicious food and the bread, which she had prepared, into the hand of her son Jacob.

So he went in to his father and said, "My father." And he said, "Here I am. Who are you, my son?" Jacob said to his father, "I am Esau your firstborn. I have done as you told me; now sit up and eat of my game, that your soul may bless me." But Isaac said to his son, "How is it that you have found it so quickly, my son?" He answered, "Because the LORD your God granted me success." Then Isaac said to Jacob, "Please come near, that I may feel you, my son, to know whether you are really my son Esau or not." So Jacob went near to Isaac his father, who felt him and said, "The voice is Jacob's voice, but the hands are the hands of Esau." And he did not recognize him, because his hands were hairy like his brother Esau's hands. So he blessed him.'

Here we see the cunning of Jacob: by clothing himself in his brother's apparel and disguising his skin to be more hairy, he received their father's blessing due to come to his older brother. In Christ we now feel like him, smell like him and remind the Father of him so he likewise places his blessing on us who are in Christ. However, this is not by trickery and deception but by Christ offering us a share in his inheritance and the blessing due to him.

Both of these stories helped me as I walked and began to pray on the beach that day. How? Well in Hebrews 5:7 we are told:

'In the days of his flesh, Jesus offered up prayers and supplications, with loud cries and tears, to him who was able to save him from death, and he was heard because of his reverence.'

Jesus prayed fervently. He was always full of faith in prayer; persistent, passionate and disciplined. He prayed perfectly, fasted and obeyed. I am in him and it is he who qualifies me. He covers me and my failure and enables me to pray, qualified by the benefits of his obedience. I hide in him like Jacob hid in Esau's clothes. I gain strength from him like Elisha putting his hands on weak Joab. So I am victorious, even when my flesh fails to reach the standards I set for myself. The effect of this was that I started to pray with faith on the beach.

I brought to God the promises of his word and began to intercede. I grew in confidence that I was being heard through the merits of Christ in which I was now standing. Rather than this having the effect of making further decisions to have days of fasting and prayer unnecessary, it had the opposite effect of making me more drawn to the one who qualifies me even when faced with my poor frail efforts! In short because I win whatever, this knowledge becomes more attractive than even cheese and biscuits! We often fail, not because we do not try hard enough but because we do not grasp just how ridiculously scandalous the grace of God is to the undeserving.

1 John 1:8-9: *'If we say we have no sin, we deceive ourselves, and the truth is not in us. If we confess our sins, he is faithful and just to forgive us our sins and to cleanse us from all unrighteousness.'*

Even as we make progress in the Christian life we will continue to find from time to time our flesh is not 100% mastered. We must not say: 'we have no sin', for it is wrong to make that assessment. But there is an ongoing flow of the water of life cleansing us as, through confession of sin to God, we dip the 'outside of the cup' of our lives again and again into the stream of forgiveness. We find the dirty marks get removed with continuing power and increased beauty as cleansing freely, endlessly flows.

6 *A change in motivation*

Learning to swim
Should be approached
With confidence of success
To lessen the chance of drowning

In light of what has already been achieved through Christ, it might seem reasonable to question how much it really matters if fresh dirt gets put on the outside of the cup. If we sin after being saved, does it need confessing or can it be ignored? And after all, some dirt on the outside will surely make the inside appear all the cleaner! This is not a new argument, for Paul revealed that some claimed his teaching gave encouragement to keep on sinning. By doing this, the contrasting cleanliness on the inside, the amazing beauty of God's grace to forgive, would receive maximum attention.

Paul indignantly denounced such a travesty by issuing a reminder that God not only dwells in the highest heavens but also within us. When we appreciate that God has made us clean as a gift of grace, it should not provoke a careless attitude to sin. Being forgiven will not lead to thinking that how we live doesn't matter as no difference is made to our standing.

We have died to sin as Paul says, so how can we keep living in it? An apple tree does not produce pears. If it does, it is not an apple tree at all. This simple truth echoes in our lives when we say we know the Lord but the fruit produced does not reflect this. If certain things accompany salvation, as the writer to the Hebrews notes as evidence of a person being born again, then the root producing the fruit must be questioned when such things are missing.

Gratitude will permeate the life of people who have realised their own need to be holy. They understand their inability to achieve this and will be of humble heart as they accept God's grace in making them holy. How and why God should have done such a thing should constantly be a daily reference point they refer to with varying degrees of illumination as they grow in Christ. Indeed, our hearts are melted by appreciation as we get fresh insights of his love and grace through scripture and by the Holy Spirit teaching us. We do not become hardened and consider ourselves to have been 'let off' with freedom to continue offending.

This appreciation produces neither careless living nor legalistic attempts to self-justify ourselves. I have had occasion to talk to people who believe that they can measure their spiritual maturity in Christ by the depth of repentance they feel over sin as it occurs. This 'repentance' continues to guarantee not only that they are genuine in faith but that they are truly making progress. Both of those routes are unnatural and inappropriate to the heart won by grace and we have seen their impotency. Rather the humility of heart produced by appreciation of grace as we 'see him as he is' and 'us as we were' stimulates an ongoing desire to please him and offer ourselves to him in love as a fragrant sacrifice to him.

Surely it is the reality of our faith in Christ and our repentance for sin that is the acid test of our true state before God. Some have more conscious awareness of things they need to repent of, particularly when undergoing a dramatic change in lifestyle. When a sinful woman wet Jesus' feet with her tears, he pointed out that those who have been forgiven much are the ones who love much. Alternatively, a young child may have grown in a Christian family and become a believer from an early age. Perhaps the child may have repeated the step on several occasions, as grace and further light dawned from hearing the gospel. Such a person may not have had the dramatic 'Damascus Road' experience that Paul encountered when godlessness was confronted in a savage and deep way. Nevertheless, the reality of repentance can still have been known and Christ embraced by faith in his finished work.

If depth and acuteness of feeling in repentance becomes our benchmark for assessing true conversion to Christ we can find ourselves soon making an idol out of it and worshipping our own attainments in it. It then becomes the very thing we are to turn from: a 'god' we have made in our own image to worship, a 'god' of our own making. Even faith and repentance are a gift from God and so we should not seek to be Godly merely to gain satisfaction from knowing that we have behaved in a correct way. It is most dangerous to pursue godliness as a means of proving to ourselves that we are genuinely born again. Such motivation to outward acts of righteousness as justification, panders to pride and self-righteous leaning. This draws the believer away from reliance and worship of God to worship and reliance on self and what has been attained. Surely, our inspiration for holy and Godly living and likeness is not aspiration to achieve a standard, but inspiration drawn from seeing true godliness in the flesh in Christ.

Does sin still need confessing?

We read in Hebrews 8:12, *'I will remember their sins no more'.* By declaring this, God affirms his satisfaction with the work of Jesus as a complete and sufficient atonement for all of our wrongdoing. Once we are 'in Christ,' our past sins and sinful nature are counted as 'dealt with' and 'in the past'.

Is current and future sin therefore automatically forgiven and not something we should give time or reflection to? Some current teaching even discourages confession of sins in the life of a believer as we are new creations, no longer under any condemnation. To answer this requires an appeal to a variety of Scriptures. To build clarity on doctrine or practice, there are some principles that help us. 'Scripture interprets scripture' - if one Scripture appears a bit vague or unclear in exactly what it means, we should find other scriptures which talk about the same subject and bring them alongside to compare and illuminate further.

Luke 11:1-4 brings insight where we find the disciples struck by Jesus' relationship of intimacy with his father. No Jew had ever called God 'father' in a personal intimate way. Yet here was Jesus modelling an affectionate and close relationship with his heavenly father. This pursuit of intimacy with God was no doubt one of the reasons why the disciples asked Jesus: 'Lord, teach us to pray'. They did not want another religious duty as most of them had been brought up with the Law and all the rules and regulations of religious life prevalent in the day. No, this was a pursuit of genuine relationship with God.

In answer, Jesus did not issue a creed-like statement to recite. Nor was his answer meant for them alone but was a model for all his disciples then and now to follow. Most significantly, for the question we are looking at, was the inclusion of a request to 'forgive us our sins'. Clearly these sins are on-going and accumulating as he links it also with daily bread and forgiveness of those who sin against us. In the context of daily living, Jesus anticipates there will be occasions when his followers will need to ask God for forgiveness of some particular offence.

1 John is also relevant. It has been said that parts of this letter were aimed at those who as yet had not believed the gospel. Therefore the appeal is 'confess your sins', the inference being that once you have done so, there is no longer any need to continue to confess sins. The problem with this is that

Chapter 2 makes it clear that John is writing to Christians. He is encouraging them that not only is there initial forgiveness for sins but also ongoing provision to appropriate, should they find themselves having committed more sin. Verse 1 reads *'My little children, I am writing these things to you so that you may not sin, but if anyone does sin….'*

Likewise the phrase *'if we say we have not sinned'* (1 John 1:10) shows clearly that living in a state of either sinless perfection or dismissal of sin is neither appropriate nor realistic. John anticipates that mature Christian living will encompass the fact that we have sinned, do sin and will sin. Not by desire or wilful determination, but through the weakness of the flesh from which as yet we have not been redeemed. However this does not mean living with constant guilt about our sins as 'we have an advocate' (1 John 2:1).

We will sin even as Christians! It's perhaps best not to wait until we have a planned prayer time before we ask forgiveness for a harsh word, or unkind thought, or lustful look. It is also unfruitful to trawl our minds trying to find and recall sins we might not have confessed. Better in the absence of a guilty conscience to say to the Lord: *'See if there be any grievous way in me and lead me in the way everlasting'* (Psalm 139:24). Asking God to show us is wise – he will! The point, though, is that we should expect from time to time for issues and sins to come up in life that we need to bring to God, to confess and ask for grace to avoid in the future.

Confessing to one another

'Confess your sins to one another and pray for one another that you might be healed' James 5:16

Here we find encouragement that we need others to be involved in our recovery from the effects of sins. There will be occasions when such confession will aid our walking free from habits, snares and strongholds, false guilt and condemnation. Even though our sins have been forgiven, we may still carry unnecessary shame and need to confess sins to others who can help us truly leave them behind.

This is not like some sort of confessional! But it is at times helpful and powerful for people to pray over us and pronounce in agreement based on Scripture that we are forgiven. I have seen this powerfully help people trapped in the prison of their thoughts about what they had done and who could not accept forgiveness. The involvement of others at such times to bring perspective, anointing of the Holy Spirit and accountability to the process is vital. Again such a verse being in Scripture indicates that Christians will face times of sin that need effective handling.

What was Jesus like to be with?

I have often considered this question during my Christian life. How did he talk to people? What kind of a personality did he have? I only caught a more vivid and crisp view of the answer to this once I realised that the admonishments from the epistles towards a certain kind of behaviour are peppered with simple encouragements to be like he was. So for instance:

Titus 2:7-8: *'Show yourself in all respects to be a model of good works, and in your teaching show integrity, dignity, and sound speech that cannot be condemned, so that an opponent may be put to shame, having nothing evil to say about us.'*

Titus 3:1b-2: *'Be obedient, to be ready for every good work, to speak evil of no one, to avoid quarrelling, to be gentle, and to show perfect courtesy toward all people.'*

These texts along with many others in the epistles show us what Godly character looks like. There is no abstract moral code concocted by God to keep us in line and without any reason, other than it is just the way that God wants it to be. Rather, these verses show us up close what it must have been like to be with Jesus. He would have exhibited all these qualities in abundance and consistently. This would have made him such a joy to be with, such security and peace being around him. No edge to him, no hidden agenda, no false front. Imagine it, day after day! To be with a person who was a 'model of good works', full of integrity and dignity in all he said and did, all the time!

He never quarrelled, had an edge or acted selfishly. He never tired of your company; was always gentle and servant-like in how he handled you; was always wonderfully courteous in the presence of others. His 'sound speech' meant his words commended themselves, bringing wisdom, peace, affirmation and security. They conveyed a sense of being loved and cared for, being known and understood, believed in and supported. No wonder Peter protested 'No, not the Cross for you!' Was this the ranting of a man trying to hinder God's saving plan? Rather, a man who'd been won by perfect love that he could not bear the thought of it being taken from him. Everything about Jesus' personality and behaviour brought the utmost rest and joy and peace into the lives of those around him. Peter had God around on a daily basis. God incarnate – Emmanuel God with us. His motivation was 'I cannot imagine what it would be like to have this wonderful man removed from constant companionship'.

A change in motivation

Jesus is not some impersonal ransom given for us. He is no brave but anonymous soldier giving his life on a distant battle field. His bold sacrifice may have gained our freedom but it has also introduced us to his person and given us love for him. Jesus is not to be for us like some anonymous ransom for which we are grateful but detached. God has paid the price for our forgiveness and this work on our behalf is effective to clean and forgive all who access it by faith. Notice Jesus said to Peter, 'Do you love me?' He did not say 'Do you love what I have come to do?' nor even 'Do you love the things you have been seeing me do?'

We love a real person. God came near to man to reveal God's heart, character and nature to us in full. We can listen to him, touch him, be intimately acquainted with all it means to walk daily with a person who in his earthly life personified all Titus encourages us to be like.

We aspire, then, to be like him as he has inspired us. We love a real person with real characteristics and the more we see, the more lovely he becomes to us. Grace to be Godly flows from this most pure and only acceptable form of hero-worship. What a magnificent man he was and is to be around. I want to be like him. This is where grace motivates us to say 'no to ungodliness'. Its focus is not on legalistic ticking of boxes to be acceptable to a grumpy God. Our motivation should come from inspiration to be like the one who I can see lived out these attributes. To be Godly is to be like Jesus.

Cleaning up the flesh

Our attitudes, habits, emotions, appetites, aspirations and leanings, in all their complicated and fallen facets, need to conform and arise from a desire to be like Jesus. This is what makes us truly useful to his purposes. As Robert Murray McCheyne said, 'It is not great talents God blesses but rather great likeness to Jesus'. 5

He who would make a big impact for God in his day must put prime store in being more like Jesus rather than developing skills, strategy and ability to gain ground in enemy territory. The devil hates a Godly man and hated Jesus for this reason. Rather sobering are the words of Jesus that to follow him means to share in his sufferings. These arise because godliness is a powerful force in the world that attracts opposition. Nevertheless, an army of people inspired by their captain, not by fear of his power but by adoration of his example, will always command a following.

Surely the attractiveness of our future home, when heaven breaks in and earth and the heavens are remade in purity, when the glory of his kingdom is manifested in fullness forever, is that we shall be with him! It's not just about enjoying the personal benefits of a universe made perfect, with the effects of the fall removed in some kind of selfish isolation from God. Above all else, our desire is to be with him and to enjoy his company.

I have had the privilege in my life to meet people who remind me of Jesus. Something about their life and character is so magnetic that to be in their company is a delight to be savoured and eagerly anticipated. Even a phone call lifts the heart. No wonder Paul said 'Put off therefore whatever belongs to your earthly nature'. It is natural for the new nature to want to do this. Having Christ's nature shared with us can only result in a longing to be like him. It is 'deep calling to deep', a craving to be near him, to be like him.

Only in this context of love and pursuit of relationship with one who has captured our hearts and affection can we possibly make sense of Paul's exclamation in 1 Corinthians 9:27: *'I beat my body and make it my slave'.* What does he mean? He is demonstrating a healthy Christian attitude, formed out of love for Christ, not to let anything gain mastery over him and thus win his affections away. Anything that draws, captivates or entices me so that my love, satisfaction with and devotion to Jesus is compromised must not be accommodated. This is what Paul is ruthlessly expressing an intention for. It is the normal response of a heart won by love to 'make it my aim to please the Lord'. Not because I have to, but because I love him and want to. He has won me by who he is.

Grow in Grace

Consider the emphasis Paul puts in Ephesians 4:17-32 where he talks about putting off things that are to do with the old life. If you bear the illustration of the four cups in mind, when reading this passage you can see how each cup comes into play. He exhorts us no longer to walk as Gentiles do in futility of thinking. They are darkened in their understanding and that is not the way we learned Christ. We are taught in him to put off the old self, to scrub the outside of the cup, to clean ourselves up. Our old nature and consequent behaviour was sinful but now we have a new nature, a cup clean on the inside. So let us make our behaviour, the outside of the cup, match the inside.

Grace does not lower the standard for how we live. Rather grace means there is no standard to keep to be justified, because it's a gift. Grace fully accepts Christ as saviour and empowers us with the gift of a clean heart. We do not have to sin anymore; we don't have to go down that old road of filthy behaviour because that's not where we are being driven. No more are the engines in our lives producing that which defiles us. Once in Christ we have a new nature with a genuine desire to please God.

Does this mean we can be sinless? Sadly the extent to which our bodies have been corrupted means that it will take the rest of our lives to deal with and more. Full redemption will not take place until our bodies are glorified when Christ returns. When this happens our bodies will finally have caught up with our nature. Until then, the pull of the appetites and desires of unredeemed flesh will affect us.

Yet we do not have to sin; the destructive generator that was in our hearts has ceased production. No longer does it feed the flesh with fresh ways to satisfy the appetite for sin. In Christ we now have a clean generator that wants to love God. But there is just the unfortunate encumbrance of the flesh that still insists it wants its own way. Now however I say to myself 'No! I am not going to watch that television programme' whereas before I would be down every sort of avenue looking for some sensuality. Now I have the power to say I don't want to do that and I'm not going to do it.

Grace doesn't trivialise sin as if it doesn't matter; this is not grace, for the application of grace strengthens us! Titus 2v12 says *'the grace of God helps us say no to ungodliness,'* so it's actually knowing you are clean that produces the ability to stop sinning, which is totally the other way round to how many churches teach it. Some mistakenly teach 'You must sanctify yourself in order to be pure before the Lord'! This is unhelpful. We have been made clean, so we stop sinning because it is not who we are! If we live by rules we will become Pharisees. If we don't give ourselves any aspiration to want to please the Lord with the flesh, we will be sinful.

The following chapters examine in detail how being motivated by grace can help us practically in many different ways. Living under grace means so much more than knowing our standing with Christ is secure. Grace can transform every area of life, from our patterns of normal behaviour through to the miraculous. The Holy Spirit is sent not only to help us in our weakness but also to demonstrate the advancing of God's Kingdom. Grace is needed to help us use scriptures as they are intended: as spiritual food that illuminates the wonders of God and as deadly weapons to rebuke our enemy the devil. Grace teaches us how to pray effectively, to give generously and receive joyfully when in time of need. It is by grace that the life of a believer goes into turbo charge and becomes dangerous to those who oppose God. Yet by greater measure, grace helps us to reach out and aid the poor, the needy, the sick and the oppressed.

PART TWO

APPLICATION

7 *Grace to live a Godly life*

How can a correct understanding and application of grace affect the quality of our lives? In John 10:10, Jesus offers *'life to the full'*. Titus 2:12 states *'the grace of God teaches us to say no to ungodliness'*, while Hebrews 13:9 says *'it is good for our hearts to be strengthened by grace'*.

Legalism, religious observance and rules serve only to mask underlying heart traits. Even if the rules are kept, only pride will result, whereas failure will cause condemnation. If understood rightly, Grace does not produce weak, sinful Christians but rather believers living fulfilled lives who grow in wisdom, making right choices and avoiding sin. Grace provides the fuel to strengthen the heart to walk in faith.

Where the 'rubber hits the road' in the Christian life is not so much in the Sunday morning church service or the midweek cell group, but more on a Monday at work in an office environment of gossip, back-stabbing, unfair treatment, pressure, stress and deadlines. The teacher stands alone before an unruly class while the businessman contends with falling sales, hard decisions over employee jobs and the threat of financial worry. The nurse comes under pressure to be more efficient even with more patients to care for than time will allow. This is the 'stuff' of life.

At home, we may face challenges in marriage as issues occur. Tension grows in raising children in the right way and our minds are attacked with all sorts of questions and concerns. In all of these areas, the things we say, think, feel and do make a huge difference to how we live and how much the Lordship of Christ really is over everything in our lives. With so many potential pressures some people conclude: 'let's not bother with responsibilities; live life free and loose'. If you never grow up, you need never be responsible. Failure to take responsibility is one of the greatest challenges to Christian maturity.

We can think sin is when we do something wrong. However, it can be just as offensive to God for us to not do something we should have done as to find ourselves gripped in some wrong behaviour. 'Transgressions' are when we step over a boundary and do something wrong and thereby commit sins of 'commission'. To sin is from an old Saxon word meaning to miss the target, or more precisely, to fall short of the mark. Sinning is failure to take responsibility; an 'omission' of not doing what we should have done. The word 'Sloth' which in Christian moral terms has historically been seen as a sin, is defined as spiritual or actual apathy. It is putting off what God asks you to do, or not doing it or anything at all. Other words for the same thing are 'Acedia' which is a Latin word, or from the Greek language we have 'ἀκηδείᾱ', meaning 'Carelessness'. Sins of omission are withdrawal, passivity, avoidance of personal responsibility to act or behave in a certain way.

Missing out

Another sobering thought is that failure to take responsibility can mean stopping short of taking faith-filled risks. How is faith to be put into practice when believers do not speak up or stand out in serving God, nor make a stand against injustice? People can be afraid to study in case they fail the exam, get married in case it doesn't work out or take promotion in case they cannot handle the pressure. Of course, wisdom is required in making decisions but that is not the issue for many. It is more when wisdom and counsel from Godly people encourages them to progress that they back off, unwilling to bear the weight of a responsible decision.

This is more and more prevalent in these days, when it seems courage and personal strength are in short supply. Too many Christian fathers leave the disciplining of children to their wives; some Christian women never develop Godly character, that makes them attractive and potential marriage partners to Godly men looking for more than skin-deep beauty.

It is just the way I am

In the Old Testament, both Ezekiel in 18:1-2 and Jeremiah in 31:29 comment on a proverb common in the culture of the day. It seems to emphasise passivity and lack of personal responsibility for how we behave. The proverb reads: *'the fathers ate sour grapes and the children's teeth were set on edge'.*

The implication is what has been done by others has made me how I am! Both the prophets speak against this proverb. They agree that we are not in control of ill treatment and, true enough, people can at times treat us badly. However the point is that we remain in control of our actions and must take responsibility for our response to whatever has been done against us. Consider that the vile sins we suffer draw more mercy and compassion from the heart of God in our favour. As a result, perhaps, we are less likely to repeat these crimes. So if your father used to drink too much and beat you, it's not inevitable that you are going to do the same thing to those you love.

You and I are responsible for our own behaviour. It's common in our culture to hear people blame circumstances, parents, ex-partners or the government for how they are behaving. Our flesh needs to be subject to the Lordship of Christ. Modern psychology might say we are products of our environment, mere circumstances of birth. We therefore can't help sinning because of what has been done to us or what has shaped us. The cross is bigger than psychology! If the same power that raised Christ from the dead is at work in us who believe what the Bible says, then all our fallen and dead sinful behaviour and conditioning can be transformed and liberated by the power of the risen saviour Jesus Christ. We can change because of the Cross before which all sinful behaviour is forgivable. Furthermore, all lives are able to be redeemed and restored through the power of the Holy Spirit by the grace of God. If this was not so, if there were cases beyond the reach of God, then the cross would be limited in power. Something more in the universe would be needed, greater than the love and power of God and more powerful than the atoning sacrifice of Christ. There is nothing greater.

Responsibility in repentance

We have to meet Jesus at the cross as responsible people who have sinned. We are forgiven when we confess and repent of our sin; not make excuses. Only by realising we deserve just judgment from God because of the sin for which we are responsible, can we find true biblical forgiveness through biblical repentance. Repentance is not remorse, as that is feeling sorry about something but not sorry enough to change. A husband committing adultery might be sorry, but it's sorrow he got caught and that everything is now in a mess. He may not be sorry for sinning nor accept he is completely guilty. Neither will he change and accept the consequences for wrongdoing without blame-shifting.

Repentance flows not from seeing what we did wrong but from seeing what we could have gained had we lived correctly. What should follow is sadness with a conviction to acknowledge waywardness. We will want to turn towards the right way to live, a way that is both pleasing to the Lord and actually brings us deep personal satisfaction.

Forgiving people

While we are not responsible for bad things done to us, we are responsible for how we react to these events. When we take personal responsibility for forgiving those who have wronged us, real and lasting freedom becomes possible. Someone you have forgiven can't hurt you any more. You now have the power to be in control of your own actions and reactions. Forgiveness begins as a responsible decision taken through an act of will. Feelings in due course will take a lead from such decisions as these. I have known people who decided to forgive and for months, even years, had to keep restating that fact: they'd decided to forgive. They had to battle to keep the ground of 'decision hill' as it faced repeated assaults from 'bitterness army'. Eventually all battles on this area are won and feelings follow the repeated stands taken by us through grace.

Distorted by opinions and words of others

Why is it that some people do not take personal responsibility for their lives? Well, some people have been spoilt in their upbringing by doting parents, who, think they are helping by allowing no 'life' experience, no initiative and by giving no correction. In fact they are inoculating their child against growing up! Or conversely, some people receive so much criticism that they are scared to try anything for they are convinced it will only result in failure. Repeatedly, they've been told their brother is more skilful or their sister is more intelligent. If people think they are never good enough, they will always find it hard to take responsibility for fear of failure.

What has this to do with grace?

Everything! When faced with a time of extreme personal pressure, Paul revealed that he had asked God three times to take something away from him, only to receive the reply,

'My grace is sufficient for you, for my power in made perfect in weakness' (2 Cor 12:9). Like Paul we can face pressures in life so demanding that we too must repeatedly ask God to deliver us from them. At times the answer is quick and liberating. At others we find ourselves facing an illness that will not budge or a long-term trial. We can have prolonged periods of restrictions. Grace enables us to resist temptation to relieve pressure temporarily through sin, escaping reality by stimulating our bodies and minds with sex, alcohol or other self-indulgent passing pleasures.

The grace of God is enough for every difficult situation. It can be found every day. Tomorrow's grace will not be here today, but tomorrow. No wonder when we look for it too soon, we start to worry. But when tomorrow comes God will show up like he promised with an ample supply to get us through the day. We will find we are reigning in life through the place in Christ where we are already standing firm.

People who take responsibility are well-placed with God's grace to have lasting marriages and successful businesses; they can make good husbands, wives and parents. Grace is available for these things. Church history shows us people who championed the cause of the poor or the suffering. Those who stood up for doctrinal purity or gave their lives in the proclamation of the gospel saw church growth in new nations. Were these people extraordinarily skilled or gifted? Sometimes, but mostly they were people who had learned simply how to draw on the grace of God. They understood the secret of living a dependent life on God and his rich provision of grace for every need. God loves it when people who feel weak still rise and take responsibility in the things he has called them to do. They have learned as the old saying goes, based on Isaiah 57:15, that: 'The highest heavens and the lowest hearts are God's chiefest dwelling places'

How does Grace come to us?

Paul's desire was that every Christian would be 'mature in Christ' and 'live by the Spirit'. Grace has this effect over time. Through grace we can become strong in the Lord and walk and live by the Spirit. As a consequence, our actions will evermore conform to Christ's likeness as we are 'transformed from one degree of glory to another' and 'transformed by the renewing of our minds'.

Ephesians 3:16 gives us an example of how this principle might work out that 'according to the riches of his glory he may grant you to be strengthened with power through his Spirit in your inner being'.

We can see from this it is God who works in us by grace through the Holy Spirit as we seek and listen to him, yield and work with him. This ultimately causes us to grow strong in the Lord. Samson achieved more than an ordinary man by the grace of God. We receive grace by the Spirit through prayer and not by working or earning God's activity or interest in us. We might wonder why God should answer such a prayer for the Spirit to come and strengthen us.

The answer is that Christ secured the Holy Spirit's interest in your life and mine. This flows from the 'riches of his glory'; God is rich in grace towards us. He has the capacity to change us out of his riches freely given to help us. The purpose of receiving these riches of grace is that you may be 'strengthened… in your inner being'. As the subsequent verse in Ephesians 3 then points out 'to be able more and more to grasp the breadth and depth of the riches of God's love'.

This strength from God, given by his grace means we become able to do more than we would naturally; to withstand pressures others would look at and wonder: 'how do they do it?' Grace does this. Grace is by God coming to us in the person of the Holy Spirit. I emphasise this particularly so we are not left believing that grace is some 'mind trick,' where we start to think positively or train ourselves to be different. We cannot achieve the heights grace can take us to through human effort. No, it is God who comes to us. I have seen people face huge personal trauma and remain strong in their life through a daily visitation of the Holy Spirit bringing them fresh daily grace. God does this. Who can bear patiently when wrong has been done to them? Who can find themselves able to stand under the weight of many afflictions? Surely it is the person who is grace-taught and grace-fed by the Holy Spirit.

This same grace enables all our faculties; emotions, will, temperament and thought-patterns to work together in maturity. Like when fixing a broken clock, all the cogs are put back together in the correct functioning order. There is no 'stiff upper lip' but rather a melted and subdued soft heart of love that beats with dependency and trust in Jesus.

We co-operate with God in these things. We can choose to worry, fret and deny access or application of the grace of God. Colossians 3:2 reminds us *'Set your minds on things that are above, not on things that are on earth'.* This is our responsibility. God will not directly change how we think, rather he will give us grace to change how we think. As we step out, rather like Peter on the water, we find another power at work that when we look back we cannot understand how we made it with such wholeness. It is not just a case of 'let go and let God' as this is like a ship without a rudder and just living as we feel would be a recipe for disaster. The Bible encourages a proactive stance from us. Philippians 2:12-13 says: *'work out your own salvation with fear and trembling, for it is God who works in you both to will and to work for his good pleasure'.*

These verses show the two wonderful angles of the Christian life. God has and is still doing the work to save me as he planned and purposed and will continue to complete this work. I am responsible to work out this salvation by fully co-operating with God to become a more Christ-like person in thought, word and deed.

Putting on putting off

Simply put, we have to adjust our lifestyles to accommodate the enabling power of the Lord. Ephesians 4 says: *'if we have been stealing, then steal no longer'* It does not happen automatically and we might still be tempted in our flesh.

The fact is not just that we have the same Holy Spirit power that raised Christ from the dead at work in us; it's that we can say no to sin and thereby change. We are responsible for doing so and enabled by grace to know our righteousness is an unchangeable fact. This empowers us in freedom to live as sons and daughters of righteousness. We should now have nothing to do with the fruitless deeds of darkness; we are now light in the Lord: it is black and white.

Living for the right agenda

Jesus loved obeying his Father. It wasn't hard or irksome for him for he said: 'I delight to do your will' and 'I have come to do the will of him who sent me'. This is not a reluctant heart but one filled with a great appetite to please God.

Our motives and actions must be given attention. Whose agenda are we living for? James 4:13-17 reveals that living for our own agenda causes us to say: 'we will do this and then we will do that', as if we are in charge. Rather we should be seeking God's will for our lives and following in obedience. We are responsible to *'find out what pleases the lord'* (Ephesians 5:10)

This prayer of commitment written anonymously by an African Christian captures something of the zeal our hearts should seek to cultivate for the Lord and his purposes in and through our lives.

My commitment as a Christian

I'm part of the fellowship of the unashamed. I have Holy Spirit power. The die has been cast. I have stepped over the line. The decision has been made. I'm a disciple of His. I won't look back, let up, slow down, back away, or be still.
My past is redeemed, my present makes sense, my future is secure.
I'm finished with low living, sight walking, small planning, smooth knees, colourless dreams, tamed visions, mundane talking, cheap living and dwarfed goals.
I no longer need performance, prosperity, position, promotions, plaudits or popularity.
I don't have to be right, first, recognised, praised, regarded or rewarded. I now live by faith, lean on his presence, walk by patience, live by prayer and labour by power.
My face is set, my gait is fast, my goal is heaven, my road is narrow, my way rough, my companions few, my guide reliable, my mission clear.
I cannot be bought, compromised, detoured, lured away, turned back, deluded or delayed.
I will not flinch in the face of sacrifice, hesitate in the presence of the adversary, negotiate at the table of the enemy, ponder at the pool of popularity, or meander in the maze of mediocrity.
I won't give up, shut up, let up, until I have stayed up, stored up, prayed up, preached up for the cause of Christ.
I am a disciple of Jesus. I just go till he comes, give till I drop, preach till all know and work till he stops me, and when he comes for his own, he will have no problems recognising me
– my banner will be clear!

Carry the right things

Galatians 6:1-5 at first sight seems to contain contradictory instructions. Firstly 'carry each other's burdens' and then 'each one should carry his own load'. Indeed, in some languages Bible translation uses the same word so it is even more confusing. The reason for this apparent contradiction though is that there are two Greek words used; 'bear' and 'phortion'

'Bear' means a load you can put down after it is carried for a while. We all at various times have loads to carry that need the help of others. To have people stand alongside us and support us through a difficult time with prayer, counsel, empathy, practical help is completely in keeping with biblical encouragements to care for one another. Pressures, sorrows, suffering and failures in life are all encountered. To have other members of God's family alongside us in such times is an essential part of the church's role and identity.

'Phortion' has a different meaning altogether and can be likened to the 'kit bag' of a soldier. Each soldier must carry his own 'load'; to pass someone else your 'kit bag' would be a serious dereliction of duty and responsibility. The implication in Galatians is there are certain things in life we are responsible to carry. They should not be passed on to someone else to do for us.

We are personally to worship the Lord; someone else cannot develop a relationship with God for you. I was once praying with a dying man and he said that upon facing God he would say he knew Mike Betts! I assured him that whilst they would know who he was talking about, it would not be sufficient to gain him entrance into heaven!

Deuteronomy 6:5 says *'Love the Lord your God with all your heart, mind and soul….'* This cannot be delegated and can mean at times having to press through, even when we

do not feel perhaps like worshipping or going to church.
Sometimes it must be done in 'cold blood' out of a sense of
taking responsibility for reactions to feelings. We need not be
shaped by feelings but by Godly thinking and by responding
positively to biblical encouragement.

Consider a person having a tough time who thinks
'someone should come up and encourage me' but only finds
disappointment. Rather than looking for comfort, a much
better approach is to take responsibility to do for others what
we would have done for ourselves, regardless of whether
we receive it or not. We should be generous with our time
and possessions when others are in need. We should take
responsibility for honouring the Lord with our wealth and all
we have. This is something we must do. It's the same in serving
in the church. We can think 'someone else can do it this time,
I'm always doing it'. However, our responsibility before God is
for what we do and not what others do or fail to do.

Galatians 6:7-9: "A man reaps what he sows. The one who
sows to please his sinful nature, from that nature will reap
destruction; the one who sows to please the Spirit, from the
Spirit will reap eternal life. Let us not become weary in doing
good, for at the proper time we will reap a harvest if we do
not give up."

President Truman said famously of his role as US president
'The buck stops here!' 6 In other words he was taking
responsibility for the things his role demanded of him. We
must do likewise and not blame others.

Up close and personal

I have often found in pastoral work that how people are doing
with God or in church life is affected more than anything else
by what goes on behind the closed doors of their homes.
How is their marriage, how are the kids? When these things

are not right, other things often go wrong and get blamed as guilt is projected away from the real problem areas. Sometimes the truth is simply too painful to face. There are two sorts of pain: facing up to and embracing change, and staying exactly how you are, which results in just more pain.

Both husbands and wives are to take responsibility in the home and God has given men the responsibility of being head of the home. Amongst other things this means men being charged with comforting and protecting (not stifling) their wives. It means taking the flack when things come along to cause pressures. Children must be protected, trained, disciplined and released. Husbands and wives together need to take responsibility even though the husbands take headship responsibility. Both should be involved in raising and disciplining their children and looking to God personally for their resources practically and spiritually. All the time encouraging each other, looking to initiate, communicate and keep the romance in their relationship. Both are required to make sure the other one is number one in their lives, honouring and respecting each other. Individually they need to make sure the family is 'seeking first the kingdom', releasing and encouraging each other to find and fulfil their destiny, purpose and gifting. A good question for a person to ask is: "Do I see marriage as something from which I take or to which I give". Taking responsibility means the latter.

The workplace in our culture has become a place of cynicism with largely an 'us and them' atmosphere. Taking responsibility means work becoming what we do for God rather than for our boss. Keeping this in mind should affect how we do it. We will be honest and truthful, including with time keeping. We will do what is right because it is right and with humility, submit to instruction. We will be generous, so we work to give and not to get, with a due sense of accountability to God and a perspective of eternity rather than merely short-term gain. We are responsible for leading and developing ourselves, this is why Galatians 5:25 says: *'Since we live by the Spirit, let us keep in step with the Spirit.'* God has entrusted us with this life and has things he intends us to do for him in and with it. Ephesians 2:10 points out *'For we are God's workmanship, created in Christ Jesus to do good works, which God prepared in advance for us to do.'*

How do we change?

The areas where responsibility is not being taken must be squared up to and confessed to God. Where is indifference occurring and how do we react when we let someone down? It may be helpful to become accountable to someone who can keep you on track. Start to deliberately challenge your thinking when for example you start to become passive of cynical; say to yourself 'No! I am not going down that track'. Recognize it as false and habitual thinking that is in fact wrong and an incorrect distortion of the true picture.

Jesus' life is a template to follow. We see a man like us, living in communion with God the Father through the use of spiritual disciplines. Jesus prayed, read scripture, fasted and took times of solitude with his Father. Why did he do this? It was not to make up any lack he had either in knowledge or in righteousness. It must surely have been for the joy of relationship and the strength and focus such times and activities produced.

It's the same for us. Sometimes we find ourselves failing to keep planned time set aside to pray, read the Bible and intentionally draw near to God. This can happen through preoccupation with other things, just plain sleeping through the alarm clock, or a seeming inability to motivate ourselves enough to get up! The resulting feeling may be similar to that of failing to hand in homework at school and having to stand outside the head-teacher's office for punishment. However it should be more akin to someone who has been looking forward to a nice meal only to find he turned up late and missed it. Denying ourselves time with God is indeed our loss, not our sin. God is not the kind of head-teacher who is on the lookout for weaknesses and flaws in our efforts. We come to God out of relationship which is sustained through his initiative and desire. Any time intentionally spent with God is to enhance and enjoy what is already there.

Soon we will look closely at how finding grace through spending time with God can keep us on track with where God is taking us. Keeping in touch with the heart of God enables us to worship and honour him. Psalm 139 says: *'all the days for me were planned before one of them came into being'.* God has a destiny for each life, things he has in his heart for us to do, to be fruitful for him and fulfilled in him. This destiny is planned and considered by God before our birth. He calls us to adventure into his purposes so our individual lives feed into the rich tapestry of God's corporate plans for his people, the church.

Jesus went before us and showed us how to keep on track in obeying God's purposes. He learned obedience (not that he needed correcting) as his life unfolded even from a young boy asking questions in the temple and saying 'I must be about my father's business'. He saw by faith the will of the Father for him ('I only do what my Father is doing'). He embraced in full obedience all God the Father was leading him into, even the Cross. He became 'obedient unto death… even death on a cross'.

8 *Grace to read the Scriptures*

'Do not be led away by diverse and strange teachings, for it is good for the heart to be strengthened by grace, not by foods, which have not benefited those devoted to them.'
Hebrews 13:9

The Bible is an accurate account of God's revelation to us. The writings record Jesus' life as a demonstration of how to live before God in perfect obedience and also instruct us to receive the Holy Spirit who leads us into all truth. There is no need of further revelation, as all truth essential for our faith (not necessarily our curiosity) is contained within. The Bible when handled correctly in interpretation and application is a totally accurate guide for life, to know who God is and how to live accordingly.

If we develop wrong belief on doctrinal matters or matters relating to who God is and what he has promised, it is not possible for grace to strengthen us in the same way as correct understanding.

John 8:32: *'You will know the truth, and the truth will set you free.'*

This is of course not just an ability to find truth and quote it. Even the devil can do that! It is to know and apply it so as to bring the liberating effects of absolute truth to bear on our often unreliable minds and hearts.

Psalm 119:105: *'Your word is a lamp to my feet and a light to my path.'*

Our ways are illuminated by Scripture. Everything we need to know in terms of behaviour and conduct is there. In 2 Timothy 3:16, Paul mentions that 'all Scripture is God-breathed and is useful for teaching, rebuking, correcting and training in righteousness'. Scripture demonstrates to us that anything can be handled in a God-honouring way.

It is essential therefore that whether we live in a predominately literate or oral culture, the Scriptures are opened and made known. We need to discover who God is in nature and character and what he has done and promised to do. These truths stimulate the grace of God in our lives and faith and obedience flows out of the truth that strengthens us.

We cannot grow without access to revealed truth in Scripture. The ability to access Scripture is stimulation itself to increase literacy. It is not an absolute requirement to be literate to be a Christian, as most of Jesus' early followers were not, but the more we can access, the more we can be fed and strengthened through the scriptures by grace.

The power of a promise

In 2 Corinthians 2:20 we read the following: *'For all the promises of God find their Yes in him. That is why it is through him that we utter our Amen to God for his glory.'*

Someone once questioned my calling in ministry. 'What do you think you are?' he asked. 'An apostle, a prophet, the pastor? My reply was the one I have always given: 'I am a custodian of promises'.

Early on in my Christian life, I believe God spoke and promised some things for my future. He burdened my heart to see his church affected for good in particular ways that I was to be involved with. Quite how this was to happen was left blank as was the how and when. Some things are still unclear, but I do know he has called me to be a benefit to his church. These promises fuel all I have done for God and all I still do. They have been freshly invigorated through Scripture and further prophetic words all through my Christian life.

Why is it so important to know and place our full reliance upon the promises of God in the Bible? It is simply this: that one man with a promise from God is more effective than a thousand men trying to make something happen in their own strength or persuading themselves of something they are not sure God has said.

God has often used one man. In the Old Testament, many stories show one man trusting a promise from God. David, Abraham, Gideon, Joshua, Moses, all met variously with God in often intimate walks with the Creator, and all received promises from him. These promises not only defined the direction of their lives, they assured them by faith of the outcome, enabling them to press on through challenges and apparent dead-ends to the purposes God had spoken of.

So, God does speak to individuals and to whole churches through prophetic words and these, once weighed and found to be true, should be embraced by faith. The outcome of this should be that we adjust our lives so that when we see God start to move in ways he has spoken of, we are ready to respond and maximise the impact of whatever we are called to do.

Through his word, God has given us a treasure trove of promises to take hold of and live by. Any prophetic words we might receive may be a partial view. 1 Corinthians 13:9 says *'for we know in part and we prophesy in part'.* Prophesies are not completely authoritative in the same way as Scripture but they will always be instructive and revealing in ways that sit easily alongside the principles and teachings of Scripture. There will be enough to give us a clear indication of what God is saying, doing or promising, so our response can be equally clear. When it comes to promises in Scripture, the whole earth could more easily melt away than one of God's promises fails.

God gives us grace to believe what we find in scripture by diligence. We position ourselves in thought, word and deed ready for the outworking of scriptural promise in and through us. There is a need for robust and persistent attention to the Scriptures so that we become skilled in their use, able to readily find, know and apply promises to our lives.

The lives of men and women throughout church history reveal many instances when promises from Scripture, quickened by faith and felt deep in the soul, have affected destinies. By recalling the promise 'the just shall live by faith', Martin Luther birthed the Reformation, propelling him into a pursuit of proclaiming that only through grace can we be made righteous. Embracing promises creates a passion for change. It involves God in his mercy bringing about change in us, so we become instruments capable of handling the outworking of the words we embrace. This often means allowing all kinds of discipline and pressure into our lives. He is not abandoning us but maturing us. It can feel as if we have lost God and he has let go, but the reality is that his grip has never been firmer.

Grace comes through the Scriptures

Jesus has opened up access to all the promises of God. They are now 'Yes' to us who know him and to which we say 'Amen'! Our agreement means we take action and position ourselves appropriately as those who expect something to be true. In terms of growing and maturing in God, grace is activated in our lives as we appropriate by faith the promises he has made. These promises concern who he is and what he is like in his dealings with us which are kind, merciful and tender. Moreover, through the promises of Scripture we can learn how to take our stand through grace in any situation. Where we have a promise from God it should affect our perspective, no matter what is presented before us.

Promises matter. What God has said really does matter, more than anything else. If he did not mean something he would not have said it and there would be no guarantee of it. However, once he has given his word on something it means we have the right to press our case for it to be made good. It is like a cheque filled in and signed or a word made on oath. It is a promissory note for the future. It is of huge significance to us to know what God has promised and to ensure we neither remain ignorant of his promises, nor distort or misapply them through wrong handling of Scripture.

God is sovereign and will do as he pleases when he pleases. Yet Scripture also tells us of human responsibility whereby we must believe his words and press in on them for their fulfilment and to use them as a reckoner, a guideline by which to live.

I can remember some years ago that 'promise boxes' were popular. Such a box contained small rolled up scrolls of paper, one of which would be removed and read out loud each day. Each one had a promise from the Bible, something God had given his word on. The grace of God gives us the gift of righteousness and it cannot be earned nor anything done to maintain it once received. We can and should however use all the means made available to us by God to strengthen ourselves in this grace.

Hungry for God

As a very new Christian I had a significant encounter with the Holy Spirit. Rather than this experience making me more and more hungry for further similar experiences, I found myself hungry to know more about God. I wanted to know what he was like in nature and character, what his promises were and how he would deal with me. I wanted my relationship with him to grow. This hunger drew me with considerable passion to read the Scriptures and chew them over, letting them form my opinions. Over many months of summer mornings I recall rising early with the sun and pouring over God's promises.

Even now, years later, memory of those times is fresh. I can still call to mind the fragrance of the air, the sheer beauty and joy of a new day beginning as I turned to the Bible and contemplated the Saviour. Sometimes a whole psalm would take some days to work through, as I found a promise of God or something describing how he thought, felt or would act. I even started going to work and taking with me 'post it' notes on which a verse or portion of a verse was written. I would look at it, speak it in my mind, pray over it and think about it through the day. My belief in a boundless God grew in that time, and has expanded ever since. I soon learned that alongside the Bible, all I needed was a notebook journal and a pen to allow the verse, the poetry, the prayer, the gospel account to speak and shape and give me strength. I remain convinced that this simple daily activity laid the foundation for my personal relationship with God. It also encouraged the growth of obedience to his will, to his purposes and what he calls me to now.

Today can be described as an 'instant' age full of 'sound-bites' where information is easier to access than at any time in history. This is truly wonderful, but knowing a fact and being positively affected by it are two different things. A book on the grace of God therefore is not complete without a thorough, well-grounded encouragement to all believers and seekers of God to read, learn, digest and meditate on the Scriptures. Such activity is not reserved for academics or bookworms as Christianity is not this type of faith. Although the written word is powerful in spreading its good news, the oral story tradition and the contemplative study of relatively small portions of Scripture at a time, also plays a part in the life of the Bible-believing Christian.

Start young

I suggest that children should be encouraged to memorise
the Scriptures from an adult version. Some will say, 'what
is the use of learning something too complicated to
fully understand?' My response is that as a child grows
physically, emotionally and mentally, he or she will grow into
understanding. Many children have keen memories and relish
challenges and tests. If the language is allowed to speak for
itself, the Bible will soon become part of the fabric of their
personal cultural lives, standing them in good stead through
their adult lives. Paul even said to his young disciple in the
faith in 2 Timothy 3:15:

*'… and how from infancy you have known the holy Scriptures,
which are able to make you wise for salvation through faith in
Christ Jesus.'*

Children's bibles are the groundwork explanation to stories
and illustrations. Later, Jesus himself demonstrated the value
that comes from calling to mind scriptures for every situation
that life brings up.

In the church I first attended we had a simple exercise called
'sword drill'. The Bible was a sword which we sheathed under
our arms before being given a verse in the Bible to find quickly.
We were told to draw our swords and then to 'charge' one
the verse had been located. The winner was the first to find it
and most of us quickly learned the location of Chronicles and
Corinthians and the right order for the prophets.

After many years as a Christian, there are still days when I have
to be reminded who I am in Christ. I need the daily strengthening
effect of truth washing over my world-distorted, unreal
thoughts and self-perceptions about my life and what God is
doing. My daily practice is still to read a portion of a devotional
book, something to stir my heart from what another saint has

discovered and recorded, to encourage me. I then read a portion of scripture, working through a book of the Bible at a time. After that, I record my thoughts and observations on God and his ways and promises in my journal.

Meditating on the Bible

Bible meditation is an important tool for allowing the grace of God to strengthen us. It is a call in 2Tim 2:7 to 'reflect on' and in Psalm 119:15 to 'consider'. A helpful image in explanation is that of a cow 'chewing the cud'. To extract maximum nourishment and to aid digestion, cows chew grass over and over. Bible meditation means doing the same with a passage, verse, phrase or a single word. Whilst reading the Bible in large sections can be helpful, and even reading it through in entirety has some use, to ponder a little longer over smaller portions or verses is likely to be more fruitful. We can 'chew' it over, think about it and take time to 'mull' it over. The more this is done, the more is obtained. Bible meditation is a discipline every Christian should develop as it helps us learn how to 'feed' on the word of God ourselves.

Romans 12:2 says *'be transformed by the renewing of your mind'.* This happens not by someone praying for us and imparting 'a renewing of the mind', though prayer to break strongholds of thought can be useful. Rather, this transformation is effected by the Holy Spirit working in our lives through the truth of Scripture. He applies Scripture to us as we think upon it and receive and believe it by faith. It is then we find God reshaping our thoughts and feelings.

Every Christian needs to know how to get food for life from the Bible, to avoid spiritual starvation. Bible meditation is a particular form of allowing Scripture to shape our lives. It is not emptying our minds of everything, so we are vacant. Rather, it involves filling our whole minds and hearts with truth to shape and teach and to push aside falsehoods that come disguised as appealing 'truths'.

For example, a lie we believe is often that 'God does not love me'. We know it's a lie as the Bible says he does love us. Meditating upon verses that speak of his love gives us confidence to cast aside these lies through application of truth, applied with faith and confidence in his grace. Reading Scripture always brings a choice, to either believe our own mixed up heads or to submit to what is read. Here is what some great men of God said about meditation on Scripture

'If you know the preciousness of the promises and enjoy them in your own heart, take time to meditate on them. Thinking over the hallowed words will often be the prelude to their fulfilment. Many a Christian who has thirsted for the promise has found the desired blessing gently distilling into his soul while he is meditating upon the promise. He rejoiced that he was led to lay the promise near his heart. But besides meditation on the promises, receive them as being the very words of God. Speak to your soul thus: 'If I were dealing with a man's promise, I would carefully consider the ability and the character of the man who had covenanted with me. So with the promise of God! My eye must not be so much fixed on the greatness of the mercy as on the greatness of the promiser. My soul, it is God, even your God, who cannot lie and who speaks to you. This word of his which you are now considering is as true as his own existence. He is an unchangeable God. He has not altered the thing which has gone out of his mouth or called back one single consolatory sentence. It is the God who made the heavens and the earth who has spoken. He cannot fail in wisdom as to the time when he will bestow the favors because he knows when it is best to give and when better to withhold. Therefore I will and must believe the promise. If we meditate on the promises and consider the promiser, we will experience their sweetness and obtain their fulfilment'. – CH Spurgeon [7]

'Hearing, reading, marking, learning all require inwardly digesting and the inward digesting of truth lies in the meditation upon it' - CH Spurgeon [8]

'Meditation is the activity of calling to mind, and thinking over, and dwelling on, and applying to oneself, the various things that one knows about the works and ways and purposes and promises of God...It is an activity of holy thought, consciously performed in the presence of God, under the eye of God, by the help of God, as a means of communion with God.' – JI Packer. Knowing God [9]

'God's Word is not meant to be fast food. Take time for a good long chew' - JE Yoder [10]

What is there to meditate about from Scripture?

Throughout life, personal issues and decisions arise. There are challenges in how to act and react to situations; some experiences are difficult to understand and others bring pain. The ability to recall a verse that brings assurance of the character and nature of God acts like a compass in the winds of life and enables the magnetic north of reality concerning God to be found. There are essentially three core areas for meditating upon:

Who God is

The pursuit of knowing God and his character must form the bedrock of our thinking. The more he is known, the more we will trust and rely on him, especially when the way ahead cannot be seen clearly.

Psalm 9:10: And those who know your name put their trust in you, for you, O Lord, have not forsaken those who seek you.

For any of us to trust someone, we have to know them well. God is no different. We need to know for sure who God is and what he is like in order to place our trust in him. Time spent with someone, seeing how he responds to situations and conducts himself in the world, is all part of the familiarity process. Finding his true nature is the key to trust.

Many people come to faith in Christ from abused and distressing backgrounds, where people have not acted correctly. Those who should have been kind have been cruel; they should have cared and protected but instead have exploited and abandoned. We bring our history into our Christian life and foundational questions arise such as 'Is God good?', 'Will he take care of me?' and 'Can he be trusted to keep his word?' Only the reliable and authoritative scriptures can provide the answers.

What God has done

Being aware of what God has done makes us confident that what he did before for those whom he loved will be available for us today whom he also loves.

'Then I said, "I will appeal to this, to the years of the right hand of the Most High". I will remember the deeds of the LORD; yes, I will remember your wonders of old. I will ponder all your work, and meditate on your mighty deeds. Your way, O God, is holy. What god is great like our God? You are the God who works wonders; you have made known your might among the peoples.' (Psalm 77:10-14)

Such verses are hugely helpful especially when we face challenging situations. God has done things requiring even greater help in the lives of other people in the past. He will act in the same way for us who he also loves. We can recall his acts and appeal to him to renew them in our day on our behalf. Prayer can be assisted greatly by appealing to God on the basis of his past record of activity. To reflect on his mighty past deeds stirs faith for now and gives us appropriate confidence that God will come through for us. He does not change, his power has not diminished, nor his nature altered.

Nehemiah 9:3 provides a picture of the people of God meditating on what he has done: *'And they stood up in their place and read from the Book of the Law of the LORD their God for a quarter of the day; for another quarter of it they made confession and worshiped the LORD their God.'*

The rest of the chapter is a meditation on the dealings of God with his people and the observing of his character and nature as demonstrated in his actions. What he had done showed what he was like. Meditating on the works of God reminds us that he is a rock that does not change, even though life ebbs and flows through good and bad times like the tide.

Verse 17 reads: *'But you are a God ready to forgive, gracious and merciful, slow to anger and abounding in steadfast love, and did not forsake them.'*

In turn, as we face challenging times or are aware of our failure, we can find ourselves standing next to others in the Scriptures and see that as God was gracious to them he remains gracious to us. The more God helped his people through history, the more they gained confidence to face new and even greater challenges. We can do likewise and say with David: *"The Lord who delivered me from the paw of the lion and from the paw of the bear will deliver me from the hand of this Philistine."* (1 Samuel 17:37)

What God is pleased with

Psalm 1:1-3: 'Blessed is the man who walks not in the counsel of the wicked, nor stands in the way of sinners, nor sits in the seat of scoffers; but his delight is in the law of the LORD, and on his law he meditates day and night. He is like a tree planted by streams of water that yields its fruit in its season, and its leaf does not wither. In all that he does, he prospers.'

Thinking about how God wants us to live and behave enables the making of wise choices in life. We can turn to Ephesians 5:10 to 'find out what pleases the Lord'. This comes through seeing how we should live as revealed in Scripture. Some issues are a matter of personal conscience and the Bible makes it clear that for some, a certain activity or action may be wrong. However, others their conscience is unoffended and therefore not displeasing to the Lord. Such an issue might be the moderate drinking of alcohol. Other issues are clearly taught by Scripture to be wrong. It can never be right to steal, lie, cheat or get involved in sexual immorality. Having a good grasp of what Scripture says will help us be people who do not mess up or shipwreck our Christian lives. When we need wisdom to make choices, meditating on Scripture will help us make the right decisions.

It is also the case that in our lives and interactions with people we have truth to declare in respectful, gracious, provoking yet culturally sensitive ways. How can we do this if we are not acquainted with truth thoroughly? How do we know what to say and do? How do we know what is right and wrong?

How to meditate

Buy a good Bible

Practically speaking, buying a good Bible such as the NIV or ESV is important. I also like to combine either of these with a copy of The Message which is more of a paraphrase and translation of idioms. Doing this helps to bring the warmth and feeling out of certain passages. Having a wide-margined Bible is a good purchase, as it can be helpful to read and jot your thoughts down or other verses that apply next to the section you are reading. Don't treat your Bible like a museum piece: it is a work tool! A note book, pencil and pen are all that is then needed to start feeding and gaining strength from the grace found in the Scriptures.

I am not a huge fan of daily reading notes as the principle way of feeding on Scripture as we must learn how to feed ourselves. For me it is like eating something someone else has already chewed on! It can of course be helpful to check if what we have found or think we have found is theologically accurate as if we have found something no-one else has, we are wrong!

Make it manageable

It is not necessary to be very academic to enjoy the Bible; you don't even have to be able to read very well. The big mistake that is often made is to set goals that are not realistic and leave us unable to do what was intended. We get discouraged and either give up or do it out of dry duty. Better to select a manageable goal and stick to it than aim too high and always feel unable to reach it. Remember that if you never prayed or read the Bible again God will not love you any less. This is an act motivated purely by grace to feed our relationship with God as we find ourselves drawn into a desire to know him better. The more we see of God in the light of truth, the more attractive to us he becomes.

Pray and take note

Reading a devotional book or singing/thinking of a song before turning to the Bible can help to stir thoughts and open the heart further. As you begin, ask the Holy Spirit to speak to you. I am not a great fan of sticking a finger in the pages as you flip through and reading where you stop, or dropping it on the floor and reading where the page lands open. Such throws of the dice owe more to superstition than Spirit-filled lifestyle. Having said that, I have many times found that the exact portion of Scripture I have found myself reading on a particular day has had special application either to me or in a situation or for others. The providence of God is a mystery.

A disciplined and planned approach to reading the Bible has been most helpful to me. Systematically working through a book of the Bible brings a sense of purpose. Perhaps Psalms is a good place to start as it is packed with promises from God and describes his character and nature. At the beginning of my walk with Christ I loved the Psalms and Proverbs and prophetic books like Isaiah, all of which were brimming with promises and descriptions of God. Later I realised that reading the whole of God's story from start to finish was important, to see how it all hung together and who and what happened where, when and for what reason. Many reading plans exist to facilitate this, but the one put together by Robert Murray McCheyne [11] has been very helpful to me.

After reading, reflect on the most significant verse or verses discovered for further meditation. Repeat the verse or phrase a few times, slowly, placing emphasis on each word in turn. Think, ponder, chew over and reflect on each important word or phrase. Ask key questions: What does this tell me about God and his ways? What application does it have for me today? How should this shape my life, perspectives thoughts and feelings? What should I change in my thinking or attitude right now in light of this? Record a few thoughts in a daily journal to clarify your thinking and refer back to later.

As a start, have a look at Psalm 119. This is the longest chapter in the Bible and it lists all the benefits of meditating on Scripture. Why not read it and see how the emphasis in each of the verses given help you get an idea of how to identify and meditate on key themes in Scripture.

v9–11   keeps you from sin

v14–16 makes your life full of joy

v28   lifts you up during times of difficulty

v30–32 reveals what pleases God

v41–43 gives us ammunition in spiritual warfare

v49–52 gives us a rock upon which faith can hold fast

v62   stimulates worship

v63   provides the basis for fellowship

v72   puts the value of other things into perspective

v77   reveals what God is like

v105   helps us with decision making

v120   produces a right fear of God in us

v126   helps us pray according to God's will

v136   gives us a passion for righteousness and God's honour

Time and location

Although reading the Bible regularly won't make God love you any more, it is important as it expresses to God the fact that we need him. Giving time to seek him in this way with a dependent attitude will help us grow in depth and maturity as Christians. Perseverance itself is a sign of Christian maturity, so pushing through a dry time can actually be part of God's work in your life, even if it doesn't feel like it.

Everyone will find different times and seasons of life better for them in progressing in this area depending on their own circumstances. These include time itself, family responsibilities, academic abilities and even personality. It is important to remember that you will not always feel you have achieved anything from it. However, like eating, if you stop you will soon notice the effect

The Bible shows various people with different ways of feeding on God's word:

All day long *Psalm 119:97* Try writing down verses on a card, put it in your pocket in order to meditate on it through the day, or try some memory verse exercises.

Fresh each day *Exodus 16:4* and *Deuteronomy 8:3-5* Israel received 'daily manna', the point being that yesterday's food does not satisfy the needs of today.

At the beginning of the day *Psalm119:147, 5:3* A disciplined time before being overtaken by activity is often the best approach.

In the night *Psalm119:55, 62,14* Reflecting on God's word before you sleep again can be a useful way to end the day. So where is the best place to read? Ideally, it is a place of habit where you will not be interrupted and where you can give it your full attention. Varying the location, indoors or out can help keep the discipline fresh. Make sure you have a pen and notepad to record anything God may impress upon you.

Finally, there is no short-cut to growing in God. He is full of grace in his saving of us, and he gives us grace to grow through the understanding of Scripture and in believing in his promises. This most certainly requires that we access the grace he has made available.

9 *Grace to receive the Spirit*

God's way of interacting with us is through the Holy Spirit. We are born again by a supernatural action of the Spirit which is just as much a miracle as bringing a dead physical body to life. This act of power is prompted and motivated by the grace of God towards us in Christ. God also speaks to us through the Holy Spirit. Jesus said it was good for us that he went away as then another just like him would come to teach, empower and be with us just as he had been.

Having begun our Christian lives by the Holy Spirit, the Scriptures then urge us to walk in close fellowship with him and continue in his power to work out our new life of following Christ. We were saved by grace and so must continue in grace. Our growth and service to the Lord should be motivated, directed and empowered by the Holy Spirit through grace. We must 'walk by the Spirit and then we will not gratify the desires of the flesh' as Galatians 5:16 puts it. Accessing the vast supply of ongoing grace through the Holy Spirit is the only way to live the Christian life effectively. We are dependant entirely on God yet must be responsive to him completely.

Holy Spirit and two kinds of Church life

It can be confusing for both new Christians and those still exploring to visit more than one church and find a quite different corporate expression of faith in liturgy and practice. Often this diversity is due in no small part to the perceptions and beliefs held by the leaders of each church on the role and activity of the Holy Spirit in corporate church life. These differences in theology can often be seen as expressed in two types of church practice.

There are churches that believe the gifts and ministries of the Holy Spirit such as speaking in tongues, healing and prophecy were only for the first season of church history. They claim the gifts of the Holy Spirit, as a normal and expected part of church life, died out with the first apostles. This view is often termed the cessationist view.

Some believe these gifts and ministries are still possible but are somewhat extraordinary and unusual. Leaders therefore exercise extreme caution and discourage their use. They rarely allow or seek them in church life, branding anything that seems to touch the 'emotional' side of our natures as excessive or a deception that needs to be guarded against. Instead, such churches often put emphasis on the 'fruit' of the Holy Spirit listed as in Galatians 5:22, such as love, joy, peace and patience as opposed to the gifts of the Holy Spirit for example tongues and prophecy.

The other brand of church life seems to welcome and expect the gifts, ministries and activity of the Holy Spirit at all levels, seeking to hold a Word and Spirit approach. It has to be said that not all churches embracing this approach are necessarily helpful in all of their belief and practice. In fact some are quite the opposite and even unbiblical in various aspects of belief and practice.

How did we get here?

What happened over the years to produce this polarisation was that fewer and fewer people sought the gifts of the Holy Spirit or practiced their use. Consequently fewer people expected the gifts to be a normal part of church life. When no-one expected them I believe preaching then sought to normalize and explain their absence by finding passages that explained and fitted the current experience of the church. There is a warning here that we must always preach what the Bible says even if we are not experiencing it at present. For example I cannot with integrity teach that God makes people ill or that he ever wants them to be sick. I can only find examples of Christ healing people in his ministry. I can never find him saying 'this affliction is good for your character development therefore I will leave you sick'. The reality though in life now is that I often find people are not healed. But if I twist Scripture to suit and fit my present experience, and what is often my pastoral observation, I limit faith being developed for greater things to be seen. More seriously, I actually distort Scripture to suit my own experience and observation. I would rather live with questions than change the message.

We also need to heed the warning that just by being open to The Holy Spirit we are not guaranteed to avoid other errors. The church in Corinth is an example of this, as they were very awash with the gifts and ministries of the Holy Spirit but had many issues of doctrine and practice that were in urgent need of correction and lining up with Scripture.

The Holy Spirit and two kinds of emphasis in explaining Scripture

Let us examine the interplay between fruit and gifts of the Holy Spirit. Two passages are often used to emphasise the need for the fruit over the gifts:

Galatians 5:16-26

'But I say, walk by the Spirit, and you will not gratify the desires of the flesh. For the desires of the flesh are against the Spirit, and the desires of the Spirit are against the flesh, for these are opposed to each other, to keep you from doing the things you want to do. But if you are led by the Spirit, you are not under the law. Now the works of the flesh are evident: sexual immorality, impurity, sensuality, idolatry, sorcery, enmity, strife, jealousy, fits of anger, rivalries, dissensions, divisions,

*envy, drunkenness, orgies, and things like these. I warn you,
as I warned you before, that those who do such things will
not inherit the kingdom of God. But the fruit of the Spirit is
love, joy, peace, patience, kindness, goodness, faithfulness,
gentleness, self-control; against such things there is no law.
And those who belong to Christ Jesus have crucified the flesh
with its passions and desires. If we live by the Spirit, let us also
walk by the Spirit. Let us not become conceited, provoking one
another, envying one another.'*

These verses indicate that by walking in the life of the Holy
Spirit, he will produce in us a Christ-likeness in our character
and lifestyle. Those who are nervous of the gifts of the Holy
Spirit emphasise such verses as being of more importance
than operating in gifts of the Holy Spirit.

Another portion of Scripture often quoted in connection with
this is:

1 Corinthians 13:1-13

*'If I speak in the tongues of men and of angels, but have not
love, I am a noisy gong or a clanging cymbal. And if I have
prophetic powers, and understand all mysteries and all
knowledge, and if I have all faith, so as to remove mountains,
but have not love, I am nothing. If I give away all I have, and
if I deliver up my body to be burned, but have not love, I gain
nothing. Love is patient and kind; love does not envy or boast;
it is not arrogant or rude. It does not insist on its own way; it is
not irritable or resentful; it does not rejoice at wrongdoing, but
rejoices with the truth. Love bears all things, believes all things,
hopes all things, endures all things. Love never ends. As for
prophecies, they will pass away; as for tongues, they will cease;
as for knowledge, it will pass away. For we know in part and we
prophesy in part, but when the perfect comes, the partial will
pass away. When I was a child, I spoke like a child, I thought like*

a child, I reasoned like a child. When I became a man, I gave up childish ways. For now we see in a mirror dimly, but then face to face. Now I know in part; then I shall know fully, even as I have been fully known. So now faith, hope, and love abide, these three; but the greatest of these is love.'

Some use these verses to say that love and other Godly character traits are far superior to gifts of the Spirit like tongues and prophecy and so are more worthwhile to pursue. Others say that the passage indicates that these gifts have now passed away, leaving the pursuit of likeness to the character of Christ to be our sole passion.

Neither view is correct as each set of verses in their context reveal that not only is there no biblical teaching to suggest that the gifts of the Holy Spirit have ceased but also these and other passages show that mature Christ-likeness of love, hope, joy, patience and compassion are the environment and atmosphere in which the gifts should be exercised.

The previous chapter in 1 Corinthians is all about how to use the gifts; it would not make any sense for Paul to then say 'having told you how to use these gifts, I want to remind you though that none of them are for you today'. He is in fact seeking to ensure that Christ-likeness permeates all ministry for and on behalf of Christ. As his ambassadors anything we say or do in his name should carry his likeness. He does not want power or action by way of supernatural activity in church life without it looking like it would if Christ himself were doing it. It must have the fingerprint of his character on it for it to be 'in his name'.

Additionally verse 10 talks of when the perfect comes. This is referring to the return of Christ which of course has not yet happened. When he does return the need for things like praying in tongues to tell of his glory and prophesying of his purposes to come will no longer be necessary as we shall see him 'face to face' rather than catching glimpses of his glory 'in a mirror dimly' as at present

Caricatures

This polarisation of church practice can lead to a caricature of charismatic church life emerging in the minds of those who are cautious of the gifts of the Holy Spirit. Their conclusion is that those who welcome, seek and practice such gifts and ministries tend to be immature and unconcerned with Godly character. Conversely a view can be created in the minds and attitudes of charismatics that non-charismatic church life is lacking in passion, powerless and full of empty words.

Where grace can help us walk in the Holy Spirit is in treating the gifts as from God to help us serve him. These are not earned but freely given by the ascended Christ. Grace can then also enable us to grow in maturity of character and likeness to Christ so that we represent him well in the way we minister and serve him. We need both fruit and gifts and in great measure. This is the clear application of Scripture into our generation and all future generations until Christ returns.

The environment for the Holy Spirit to work in

The New Testament indicates four key observable elements involved in the normal Christian birth: repentance from dead works and all known sin; faith in the finished work of Christ; baptism in water as a sign of being a follower of Christ; and baptism in the Holy Spirit as a 'seal' marking us as his people. These are all required for the Holy Spirit to interact with us in a way that will produce all he desires. Anything lacking is like one of the valves in a four stroke engine misfiring; the car might still move but not how it was designed to.

Our nature is changed through a miracle of the Holy Spirit. Once we were dead to God, blinded to the truth and incapable of seeing the reality of the Gospel. When we were 'born again' of the Spirit, a new heart or nature was created in us by a secret work of God only observed and identified by the fruit produced.

Baptism by full immersion into water should be done as soon as is practically possible. It shows that this new birth is a reality for us as we outwardly give testimony. As the Bible says, we have died with Christ and the water symbolises a grave that we are then laid into. Just as we only bury dead people in human life, so we only baptise people who have died with Christ. Our rising from the water shows that just as Christ rose from the dead we are also now being joined with him by a work of the Holy Spirit, having his new life as our life. We are alive in Christ and death is defeated for us. Sin no longer has a hold as we are dead in our old nature and sin cannot touch a dead man. It has no control or authority over a dead man. Baptism demonstrates that *'we have been crucified with Christ and we no longer live but Christ lives in us'* (Galatians 2:20).

There is plenty of debate over when to baptise people. Is it upon their request, even without allowing time for evidence of fruit in keeping with stated repentance? Or should we watch and wait and see if the person does in fact show through a new lifestyle that they are now genuinely changed? In the absence of specific instruction in the Epistles, we must appeal to the narrative in Scripture that reveals normal New Testament church practice.

The day of Pentecost saw several thousand people baptised and the Ethiopian Eunuch witnessed to by Phillip was immediately baptised. This seems to indicate a leaning towards immediacy upon request rather than a detailed scrutiny. The important factor is that baptism is not something to work towards once a new believer has 'grown a little bit' and proved worthy. Rather baptism in itself energizes new life and stimulates growth in Christ. It is an equipping to enable growth and make the journey, not a qualification demonstrating arrival. If possible a testing of what someone is responding to is a helpful 'litmus test'. In all New Testament examples, it is to a clear proclamation of the gospel.

Baptism with the Holy Spirit

The fourth foundational element is the 'Baptism with the Holy Spirit'. Firstly we must ensure we see what was and should be normal experience to New Testament Christians. Secondly, it is important to be better informed 'of' and therefore confident in moving 'in' the gifts and ministries available.

Grace has not only saved us but has placed us into a position where we have purpose in the Kingdom of God. Christ has a calling on each of our lives, which he planned before we were born. He desires to equip and release each of us into this and he rejoices as he sees his calling on us unfold. This calling is not going to function in all the fullness possible unless it is energised by a second receiving of the Spirit for empowerment, which is separate and subsequent to the receiving of the Spirit in conversion for salvation. The NASB gives a helpful distinction of these two events:

Ephesians 1:13-14: *'In Him, you also, after listening to the message of truth, the gospel of your salvation – having also believed, you were sealed in Him with the Holy Spirit of promise, who is given as a pledge of our inheritance, with a view to the redemption of God's own possession, to the praise of His glory.'*

Receiving the Baptism of the Holy Spirit is not automatic or unfelt; it is a sought after and identifiable event in our lives. If a person who knows what it is from Scripture is still not sure if they have been baptised in the Holy Spirit, it is most likely they have not. However, it is a promise that all can access if they so desire.

Ready to receive

Often people, whether newly saved or even after living as Christians for a while, are aware of areas of compromise and sin still troubling them in an ongoing way. It is not that nothing has changed, but rather that they wish to stop sinning in some specific areas that seem entrenched. They feel stuck and disempowered to push through. Often lack of intimacy with Christ causes a heart to remain still strong with affections for other things. Such a person might conclude 'I must get this sorted out before I can ask God to fill me with the Holy Spirit'. This is like expecting a car to drive without petrol. The Holy Spirit is required in our lives precisely to help us change and grow. We cannot do it without him. He is not a badge of achievement that some receive having progressed to a more spiritual level. He is an essential foundation to any Christian life to make genuine and lasting progress that is full and robust in its nature. We simply cannot do the will of God without the equipment of God. In grace God gives us the Holy Spirit to enable us to become all that he has called us to be and he will relentlessly and patiently work with us to achieve this.

We are promised ongoing grace in Philippians 1:6: *'Being confident of this, that he who began a good work in you will carry it on to completion until the day of Christ Jesus'.* The Holy Spirit causes us to cry out 'Abba Father', in other words he causes our relationship with God the Father through Christ to have a conscious affection and intimacy about it. This draws us not to want to sin or have any other idols in our lives drawing our affection. Repentance and change is genuinely stimulated by intimacy not by fear.

The Old Testament hope

In the Old Covenant God's Spirit was very much seen as an invading elusive visitor to God's people. It seemed that only specially selected individuals were endued with God's Holy Spirit: mostly prophets, priests and kings. However the prophets in the Old Testament looked forward to a day when the Holy Spirit would be poured out upon all of God's people, not just the select few for special tasks and seasons. Examples can be found in Joel 2:28 and Moses' prophetic desire expressed in Numbers 11:29.

The sacrificial priestly system foreshadowed a greater and more perfect age to come when Christ our great sacrifice and high priest would come and do away with the things that only pointed to his day. The day of Pentecost in Acts 2 marked a new age of the Holy Spirit and his activity amongst mankind. This new dawn was longed for by those who looked for it in the Old Testament. But only in Christ and flowing from his victory on the Cross could this new age of the Holy Spirit be ushered in. We now live in this new age where God's Holy Spirit is liberally poured out and made available for all who seek to know him. This is through grace, there are no other criteria for receiving the full measure of the Holy Spirit's activity in our lives other than that we call upon Christ our Saviour.

The New Testament reality

Acts 1: 4-5 and 2:1-17 shows the promises and longing seen in the Old Testament fulfilled. Jesus saw it as essential that his Church was endued with power from above before they undertook the commission he had given them in reaching the nations with the Gospel. If he saw it important then we must see it important.

I grew up in church environments that taught the gifts of the Holy Spirit were not for today. They were merely required to get the church off to a good start and so the Twelve Apostles were the only ones who carried this special and unique anointing. We were also sometimes taught that even if these gifts might be around today, they were according to 1 Corinthians 13 'childish things'. As we grew up in God, things like prophecy and tongues would become less important and such things would be no longer needed, not once we were able to feed ourselves more adequately on the word of God, the Bible. As expressed earlier the reality is that 1 Corinthians is not talking about gifts of the Spirit passing away now in this present age, but rather that when Christ returns there is no more need for these things, as we will see him face to face and no longer through 'a glass darkly'.

We need this power

We will not grow in God as we should without the 'Baptism of the Holy Spirit'. Over the years some have received this baptism without calling it what we would now in the light of renewed attentiveness to Scripture on these matters. Some would have had experiences they called 'sanctifying', others may not have spoken in tongues but have received the Spirit. The reason being if we do not expect and look for it, we will not do it.

I have been hugely impacted by admirable believers who would not have identified or been familiar with this baptism doctrine. Yet if they were not filled with the Holy Spirit, I do not know who is! There is though a better and clearer way forward. I thank God that I came to see Scripture rightly handled in this regard. I have seen abuse of it and excessive and unbiblical things but I would hold that the answer to abuse is not non-use but proper use. I want to model a life personally and see in my church, a community that rightly handles the word and demonstrates Spirit-led lifestyles in all ways.

10 *Grace to walk in the Spirit*

The main reference point in discovering what to expect from God the Holy Spirit is the Bible. We see that the Spirit 'comes upon' or 'fills' believers and that this experience should be an ongoing reality. Acts 2:17 speaks of a 'pouring out' while later in 8:16-17 and 19:1-6 a distinction is made between repentance baptism and receiving the Holy Spirit. In Acts 4:31and 10:45-46, believers were moved to speak the word of God with boldness and exalt God with 'tongues'.

These verses reveal a wide range of ways in which the Holy Spirit comes upon or fills us. There are a variety of initial evidences of baptism in the Holy Spirit: speaking in tongues, prophetic utterance, overwhelming joy and praise, various unusual manifestations. In fact when I listen to peoples testimonies it is rare that two are the same.

Also, there is a second experience either attending or subsequent to our conversion at which God the Holy Spirit endues a believer with power. Promises and encouragements made by Jesus indicate this to be a 'birthright' of all believers to be sought and treated accordingly. The narrative examples demonstrate it is not something that happens automatically or without us knowing.

Make it simple

Clear teaching and explanation is required concerning the baptism of the Holy Spirit in order to create an environment of faith and expectation in believers. Sometimes they need helping practically step by step, for if they do not know what to expect they are often left disappointed. I believe the whole experience mostly needs to be de-mystified.

There are several words and phrases associated with this baptism; 'filled with', 'poured out', 'receive', 'baptized with'. The word baptism means overwhelm, immerse, drench or flood; the clear implication being that something happens to us from without that originates in the Holy Spirit's activity. We do not release his activity from within initially; He comes upon us from the realm of heaven. This is something originating from God that comes upon and fills us. We receive this initiative from God by faith and then can release and pour forth from the well of his resources placed within us.

Keep it flowing

Although an initial filling is to be sought after and expected, subsequent ongoing encounters with God's Holy Spirit are also to be anticipated and longed for. Not that we live looking for experience, but encountering the presence of God in heightened ways is utterly Biblical when we consider God's dealings with individuals in both the Old and New Testament. It is completely necessary if we are to continue to grow in our knowledge and relationship with God. Personally I have found throughout my Christian life that God has met with me in new and ever increasing measures of power and visitation. I live each day longing for him in such a way. Our relationship is dynamic and continual; he is present and vital, not a distant and absent friend remembered.

Proverbs 8:34: *'Blessed is the one who listens to me, watching daily at my gates, waiting beside my doors.'*

A life filled with the Holy Spirit anticipates and longs for an ongoing breaking in of new and fresh interaction with the Saviour. This is not something earned but something supplied by his grace. Being filled with the Spirit is like a yacht continually having its sails filled following its launch onto the water. Such a dynamic example stands in stark contrast to the rather static picture sometimes used of a glass being filled with water. This latter idea can lead to passivity and reduce our expectation of receiving or needing more after we have met God in this way for the first time. We can think 'I have done that so there is nothing more'.

Receiving the baptism of the Holy Spirit

Some simple steps, practical instruction and awareness of Bible promises can help anyone who knows the Lord to come through to a genuine and clear experience of receiving the baptism of the Holy Spirit and the resultant use of gifts and ministries. It can happen even through embracing the very words you are reading and then seeking the Lord in privacy of your own room.

The foundation of repentance Acts 2: 38

Foundational to becoming a Christian is an initial turning to Christ in repentance. We must realise we have grieved him and done wrong and become aware of missing out on so much on by going our own way. How can anyone receive a saviour without realising the need for him? It is not how much depth or agony of repentance we feel that decides our genuineness (as we could end up making repentance a work), but rather the reality with which we acknowledge Christ as our Saviour and hold to him by faith.

Specific sins

Genuine repentance will mean that even after initial conversion, we may find issues that require our attention. Perhaps we did not choose to deal with them at the time or simply had not realised them to be wrong. Conversion to Christ will create a conscience sensitive to pleasing him. Ask yourself whether there is anything you are aware of that you are doing wrong or that is offensive to him.

In Acts19: 17-20 we find such an instance when believers are freshly convicted about holding onto some occult materials. Perhaps they were valuable and money would be lost, even though they did not appear to want to practice the magic arts any more. Only when this was faced and turned from did a fuller blessing of God flow into their lives. It is important therefore that all 'known' sin is confessed and turned from now. We are not to go digging to find these things as God will bring them to mind.

I have found that conviction of sin, even though painful, always brings with it a sense of relief that we can now be free. Condemnation and accusation are key weapons of the enemy. He is always vague, non specific and leaves us not quite knowing what we have done wrong or need to put right. He tries to generate a general sense of unworthiness that is not easy to remove. The Devil wants to make us feel heavy and unacceptable; he is the accuser of the brethren.

Conviction from God is not like this but rather is a precious gift of Jesus to lift us from things that displease him but are also a weight to us. Response to conviction will always leave us feeling free and relieved even if we feel pain at having our sins brought to light. God is always specific, the Devil is always vague. As I once heard said, 'God speaks to the fella in the cellar and not the fanatic in the attic!'

The foundation of obedience

Acts 5: 32 shows that as well as needing to stop doing wrong things we also need to start doing right ones. This is very much the fruit of taking responsibility. Ephesians 5:10 encourages us to 'find out what pleases the Lord'. This is a proactive task, as is Hebrews 3:15: *'Today if you hear his voice do not harden your hearts'.*

Question yourself: 'Am I aware of anything God has asked me to do that I am not doing?' It might not be something linked to sinful behaviour. Has God called you to an area of service that you are resisting knowingly? Perhaps you have been prompted to bless or forgive someone, maybe to give financially, but are resisting? We can bury God's nudges, hoping they go away. However, surrendering to Christ as Lord means he is in charge of my life, time, possessions and relationships; life's choices all become subject to his will. How can we ask for more of him when we are not giving him our all?

I often ask people such questions in praying for them to receive the baptism of the Holy Spirit. If anything needs sorting out, I encourage them to do it with determination at the next available opportunity. Grace is tough to help us be strong in sorting things out and we must 'carry our cross' as Christ did. This involves costly obedience to his will and call upon on our lives. Obediently choosing a certain path can be heavily demanding and come at a high price, all for the sake of bringing glory to Christ and advancing his cause. Jesus was 'obedient unto death' and as he, himself said, 'no servant is above his master'. Grace does not lower the standard at all. Rather it gives us power and strength to find resources in the Holy Spirit, to say no to the sin and disobedience that previously held us captive.

Believing a promise made to you

In Acts 2:38-39, Peter address the crowd: *"Repent and be baptized every one of you in the name of Jesus Christ for the forgiveness of your sins, and you will receive the gift of the Holy Spirit. For the promise is for you and for your children and for all who are far off, everyone whom the Lord our God calls to himself."*

The essence of grace is that God has done things for us that we needed to be done and should have done ourselves, but couldn't because of sin. In mercy and grace, God did them for us through Jesus and we gain access to this work by faith being placed in the personal promises of God, who does not lie. It is by grace we are saved 'through faith'. Faith takes God at his word and believes what he says to be true, even if feelings or external circumstances seem to say otherwise.

The same principle is true of the baptism with the Holy Spirit. We are told in the verse above that God has made a promise to 'all' who will believe. If we are part of 'all', then it is our promise too. Faith should mean that when we ask for this baptism there is no doubt that we will receive. We ask on the basis of a promise, a signed cheque, if you like!

How thirsty are you?

John 7:37 points out that only thirsty people drink. A casual attitude to receiving or seeking the Holy Spirit is unlikely to yield much fruit. Some people 'dabble' with the Holy Spirit. The first part of Hebrews 6 refers to dabblers: 'those who have tasted of the heavenly gift' – who live on the edges of Christian things; tasting out of curiosity or self-interest, seeing what's in it for them. Without genuine conversion or commitment to Christ they will not come back for more to find a saviour: it won't be in their heart.

The only genuine Christian experience is a passionate desire for all God has and to give to him all of oneself without reservation. Being prayed for on the basis of: 'let's give it a go and see what happens', is not a good foundation. This should matter a great deal to a believer, who knows he needs more of God and for God to have more of him. Nothing else should satisfy. Do we want all there is of God and is it our deepest desire for God to have all there is of us?

Jesus said: 'if a man is thirsty let him come to me and drink'. Only thirst is required, no other qualifications are necessary.

We may have failed and feel unworthy in many other ways, but if we are thirsty we qualify. The greater the thirst, the more eagerly the drink is anticipated and sought.

If you don't ask you don't get!

A child may look into the window of an ice cream shop and long for the wonderful flavours on display. But unless he enters and asks for what he wants, he will not receive. The same applies to receiving the baptism with the Holy Spirit. We must express to God our desire and longing. Asking shows we are thirsty and that we believe there is something to receive. It helps stir our faith as we pray out loud and make our requests known.

Some Christians can be very comfortable and assured with other kinds of prayers that 'things happen when we pray that do not when we don't'. They understand the principle: 'ask and you will receive', when it comes to all manner of requests and prayers. Yet, often when it is a personal stepping out in the belief that God through grace wants to give us the Holy Spirit in liberal measure, some find believing quite challenging.

When making a request to God, we need to ask in faith and not doubt. God invites us to ask on the basis of a belief in his generous nature and the certainty of his promises. Many, who do not receive the baptism of the Holy Spirit and accompanying gifts miss out because they are uncertain of God's willingness to give them what they ask. They have low anticipation of the abundance of the grace of God, generously apportioned to them through the qualification of their lives through Christ. I encourage people to pray out loud and simply ask for what they want. Ephesians 1:3 tells us that we have been blessed 'in Christ with every spiritual blessing'. We are 'in him' and therefore all that is his, I can freely enjoy as he shares his inheritance with me.

Pour out what you have – Acts10: 46, 2:13

Once asked for, there needs to come a stepping out in faith, usually in tongues or prophecy. Many feel initially as they start to speak that they may be 'making it up'. However, this is usually due to the newness of the gifting or an incorrect expectation of how the gift will begin to operate. Many mistakenly feel that the Holy Spirit will somehow take them over, causing words to come out, bypassing the normal use of vocal chords. 1 Corinthians 14:32-33 tells us that all gifts of the Holy Spirit are always within our control and need our cooperation to happen.

Lips and words

A picture helping people through these first steps, especially speaking in tongues, is from Terry Virgo. In the story of Elisha and a widow in 2 Kings 4:1-7, she had to begin to 'pour out' the little oil she had. As she did so, it flowed over the lip of the vessel. Supernaturally, more oil began to flow. As we begin to speak 'pouring over the lip' (of our mouth), so we will find that God the Holy Spirit will supernaturally give us more. The oil (words) will keep on flowing.

Peter had to step onto the water, physically using his legs. He wasn't lifted and placed onto the water. It took steps of faith using his normal way of walking. Similarly, speaking in tongues uses our normal way of talking and choosing/ phrasing words and sentences. It requires that we engage our vocal chords in cooperation with God, as you would initiate an ordinary conversation. Faith is speaking out in a language unfamiliar to us that we have not learned.

In reality many people make things harder for themselves than they need to. God intends and actively desires all his people receive a 'Baptism of the Holy Spirit' as part of their conversion; he is more willing for it to happen than we often are. Besides unbelief, a great hindrance is self-awareness. We can be tentative in stepping out into something new. We feel self-conscious and therefore won't step out confidently in response to the supernatural dynamic of God's activity upon us. This is often more of a problem in western nations, where logic and reason are more familiar than supernatural things. Often getting away from other people and determining to start praising God, perhaps singing worship songs, and then making a decision to start speaking in tongues out loud, is a simple but effective key to unlock our inhibitions.

A simple step with a vast horizon

When I was first introduced to the Baptism of the Holy Spirit, I was reading a small booklet in my bedroom at home. It explained things quite simply. I simply read through the scriptures listed and their explanations. I became convinced that this was Biblical and something God wanted to bring into my life to help me mature. One day, on my own and with no-one to pray for me, I simply prayed something like this:

'Lord I want everything you have for me. I believe the baptism of the Holy Spirit is a promise you have made to me in your word and therefore I say I believe your word and I ask you now to give me the Holy Spirit. Give me gifts and anointing. I believe Lord I can have access to the gift of speaking in tongues. Therefore in faith I ask and believe I have received now this gift. I am now going to open my mouth and speak in tongues trusting that what comes out will be from you. Your word promises me that if I ask you will give me the genuine thing; you will not if I ask you for 'bread" give me a 'snake' instead. I therefore, on the basis of your written promises to me, take this step of faith now in Jesus name…'

I 'chose' to pray and speak out in tongues, a language I had not learnt or heard before. It sounded like I was making it up at first, as it was completely unfamiliar to me. I had never heard these words or sounds coming out of my mouth before. They had a start and a stop and some were repeated again and again. My brain was not engaged in the choice of words as in normal communication, but was active in recognition and agreement with what was going on. The fact was, I was making these noises myself, but by faith, through my own choice of using my vocal chords, believing if I asked God for 'bread' as it were, he would not give me a 'snake'. It was an act of pure trust and faith in his promises.

After a while as I continued I felt more confident that God was enabling and owning what I was doing. I continued to do this for a few minutes, daily. I have continued to make this a daily part of my Christian life and I believe huge benefit to me and others has been caused by this simple gift of praying with my spirit rather than my mind. As I pray in tongues, I believe I am praying things that move the heart of God in ways my chosen English words simply cannot. It's another dimension. As I pray, I receive Holy Spirit impartation of grace, faith and anointing; he ministers to me answering the deep cries of my heart that I would be unable to express. To live without this gift (available to all who love Christ) is to be short-changed. It reduces the beauty of the worship we offer to the Lord; by not taking full advantage of every means he gives us to express love to him.

Growing in the gifts of the Holy Spirit

1Cor 12:1-11 gives a list of the gifts that are 'received'. They are not part of our personality but are rather distributed through the baptism of the Holy Spirit. I believe they are not a tick list of which gifts we might have, like collecting sports/celebrity/game cards as many youngsters do – "I have 'healing', have you got the 'healing' one?"

Rather these verses encourage us to see church meeting settings as opportunities to participate in the use of these gifts as God leads us. Each situation could result in anyone thus baptised by the Holy Spirit exercising them as led and provoked by Him. We should not be narrow-minded, but open to be used in any of the gifts. When was the last time you stepped out in a new way by using a gift of the Holy Spirit? The only condition attached to the use of these gifts is that they are to be used for the benefit and good of all attending – to 'build them up'. It's always important to ask yourself before sharing: 'will what I am about to say build people up?'

Tongues explained

1 Cor 14: 5, 18 indicate that the gift of tongues is available for all believers to use if they desire to do so. Tongues can be spoken or sung, individually and corporately. Acts 2: 11 and 1Cor 14: 2 reveal it as a prayer language directed to God by man and not God speaking to us. Private use is essentially for building up personally. Perhaps an overlooked aspect of 1 Corinthians 14:4 is the statement that 'the one who speaks in a tongue builds up himself'. This demonstrates the importance of the gift in enabling a person to grow in grace in a real yet mysterious way. He is made a stronger Christian and the walk with God becomes more vibrant. Such a vital gift therefore needs to be made use of regularly.

Public use of tongues

Whenever used in a congregation, the interpretation of tongues – another gift in itself – should be directed to God. It will be a prayer or exhortation concerning something about who God is or what he has done. The focus will be on him and have the effect of bringing glory to him. Sometimes, those interpreting are unclear on this and turn it round as if it is God speaking to us. In reality they have picked up the right insight but have focused it the wrong way. For example: 'I love you Lord', when turned around, becomes 'I the Lord tell you I love you'.

Alternatively, sometimes we can miss the interpretation and someone brings a prophecy which is God speaking to us and we think it's the tongue being interpreted. Good management of meetings is required to get the best out of the gifts. It's not sinful if there is no interpretation, but it's 'of no use' according to Scripture if we don't know what the person said! Public use of tongues should be managed in a meeting, so no more than 2 or 3 people (male or female) should speak before interpretation is brought, otherwise the meeting may lose order and framework – 1 Cor 14: 27-28.

Seeker friendly

Some churches have tried to hide the public use of tongues or other gifts of the Spirit, thinking that if unbelievers see them in operation, they will be put off church, concluding: 'we are nutcases'.

Indeed, it's important we make our corporate gatherings accessible to 'outsiders' who are new to Church and we are told in Colossians 4:3-6:

'At the same time, pray also for us, that God may open to us a door for the word, to declare the mystery of Christ, on account of which I am in prison— that I may make it clear, which is how I ought to speak. Walk in wisdom toward outsiders, making the best use of the time. Let your speech always be gracious, seasoned with salt, so that you may know how you ought to answer each person.'

These verses show contextualisation of the gospel is vital so we do not put people off the Christian message through our insensitivity to cultural factors. So, for example, in western society anything supernatural tends to be viewed with suspicion. Rational and logical thought processes are generally taken more seriously. However, rather than lowering church practice to what culture dictates as acceptable, we need to build a bridge for adjusting perceptions and challenging our culture with Biblical culture.

To help this, all things in church life should be done with proper explanation. 'Speaking in tongues' both builds up believers and acts as a sign for unbelievers. Scripture indicates that as they witness these gifts in operation, they will see they are clearly from a realm not of this world. This sign testifies or speaks to their consciences that they are not a part of this 'Kingdom' but another kingdom i.e. the World (1Cor 14: 22-25). To make people aware of the reality of the supernatural realm is an important Biblical goal, especially in a materialistic secular society.

On its own, tongues in a corporate meeting is usually an incomplete way of bringing people to faith, but it can be an important component, along with proclamation of the Gospel, worship and the atmosphere of love experienced by being amongst God's people.

After I initially spoke in tongues I came to see interpretation was also a Spirit-gift. I asked God to help me to do this also. I took again the same step of faith and after speaking in tongues on my own, I prayed: 'Lord, I am going to open my mouth and begin to interpret what I have just said'. I received a small glimpse of a concept and began to thank God. As I did more and more poetical and beautifully crafted sentences describing the wonder and majesty of God and his love for me flowed. I was amazed that I had said all of this. Perhaps more worship song writers would benefit from approaching things in this way!

Prophecy; another gift we all should desire

1 Corinthians 14:3 says prophecy is the revealing of an aspect of God's heart for an individual, situation or church. It should always build people up, even when it contains a measure of correction. If authentic, it will carry the grace of God within its tone and application. Further on in verses 24-25 we read that

prophecy can be directive and personalized. Verse 29 guides that in meetings, as with tongues, it should only happen in blocks of 2 or 3 before opportunity is given to weigh and assimilate what has been said. 1Cor 11: 4-5 reveals that both men and women did and can exercise the gift of prophecy (the verse in 1Cor 14: 34 about 'silent' women comes in the context of authority and control within meetings, not in the context of sharing in spiritual gifts).

Shaping my life

I can remember key moments in my life when people have prophesied to me and it has ignited faith and awareness of God's callings on my life. I have had the privilege many times of God speaking to me in such ways. Motivation to keep myself going on with God, not to lose heart, not to doubt his promises, has been kept alive and vibrant in my life through the prophetic gift.

When I was first saved we had a visiting speaker for an Easter weekend in my church. He spoke on Joseph and how God took him through various things to bring him into a place God had destined for him. Although this speaks of God's development of our character of Christ and his work in a prophetic sense, I also know God was speaking to me about my life, in some way having elements in it like that of Joseph. In that moment I felt dreams and callings and saw things in the distance I did not fully understand. I am only just beginning to now. Following this, the brother who was speaking as he left the building put his hand on my shoulder and said; 'the hand of the Lord is upon you, brother'. I cannot describe the weight of authority these words had on my life.

These same words were repeated several times by other people over the years. Each time God brought this about at a key time when I needed fresh courage to carry on. These prophetic words gave me faith that even through the long years when I was waiting for glimpses of what I had seen in my heart to come about, God was assuring me he was with me and would fulfil what he had called me to do.

Paul said to Timothy he was to remember and set his course by the 'prophecies made over you'. Individual prophetic direction might not be something everyone receives. When it is given, though, it is to be tested, weighed and, if good, held onto and attended to with the kind of attention one would give to a map or compass on a journey. Prophecy, rather than producing weak and immature believers, is essential to motivate and strengthen and direct how we live and the choices we make. We do not make things happen, we live expectant of God to bring the things he has spoken of, into being.

11 *Grace to pray*

I used to think prayer was inevitably difficult. Many preachers have quoted famous Christians to emphasise 'prayer is hard work'. Occasionally I have followed suit and found myself uttering such things when preaching. Fresh in my mind is the familiar scenario of sitting down to pray, only to realise time has gone while I stared out of the window!

I had never felt completely comfortable or convinced by books or by preachers that prayer is essentially 'hard'. Why would God make communication with him difficult? However, I assumed men wiser than me must be right; their knowledge and greater prominence meant they obviously knew better.

Prayer can at times seem hard. Our human frailties make us inconsistent and prone to distractions. Our flesh gets tired, has appetites and can be tempted by all sorts of attractive sights, touch, sounds, smells and thoughts. Moreover, verses like *'He is always wrestling in prayer for you'* (Colossians 4:12), confirm that in some instances, demanding exertion is required to pray persistently and effectively.

Like Paul, we have to take charge of our flesh and make it do as we want. One reason for fasting occasionally is to show our body who is in charge, to put our appetites into their rightful place: to curb idolatry, where we start to love and rely on something more than we do on God. Fasting reveals and challenges it. I must confess that I hate fasting! But this is because my flesh does not like to be told what to do. The appetite of my senses craves continual indulgence and satisfaction.

It is also true that prayer is a natural and pleasurable activity for Christians. Wrestling in prayer is not prayer being 'difficult' fundamentally and this is a subtle but vital point. If we carry a heart of passion for something or someone, it's not 'difficult' or 'hard' to pray about it, but it might take some effort. Exertion is required when a mountain climber wants to ascend a peak. The task will prove both 'hard' and exhilarating in the process. Prayer can be like this, especially as we will generally pray most for the things that matter most to us. The mountaineer only sets out to climb a particular mountain; he's not forced to climb but desires to - it's in his heart to face the challenge. As Scripture says, 'Where your treasure is, there your heart is also'. We must not underestimate the role of the Holy Spirit in this. A prayer list may be useful to remind us of prayer intentions, but also can make prayer seem like hard work. We pray because it's on the list and so our efforts are misdirected into avenues that at that time are not stirring the soul with genuine, God-given passion.

As Robert Murray McCheyne said: 'As surely as you did make the mouth with which I pray, so surely you do prompt every prayer of faith I utter'.[12]

The emphasis within this statement is that being led and enabled by the Holy Spirit in our prayers is vital to the flow, energy and effectiveness of them at root. Promoting prayer as a fundamentally difficult activity, only achieved by bracing oneself for action and endurance, is terribly unhelpful and fundamentally wrong. There is no scriptural warrant for such a statement; such a notion is more likely to be applauded by Hell than Heaven!

Embracing this faulty thinking is one of the major reasons why church prayer meetings are historically the most poorly attended. Who wants to go to something that one feels poorly equipped for, that is advertised as hard work for apparently little visible gain? The same principle applies to gym memberships just after Christmas. Many sign up and go for a couple of weeks, out of duty and guilt. But as the scales refuse to budge, attendance lapses and conclusion made that keeping fit is 'hard work' to no avail.

I felt God say to me some time ago that one of my greatest challenges as a leader in local church life would be to help create a culture whereby we are a praying church rather than a church with a prayer meeting. While the latter approach tacks on something for those interested in this 'specialism', the former creates an environment where the permeating culture is that prayer is normal, easy and natural. Prayer is not contained only in special meetings; not professional in style or dependant on eloquence; not ineffective but mightily powerful even when stumbling and somewhat rambling. When spoken it is born from the depths of yearning and love for Christ and his purposes.

In such an environment, a whole church community can find itself committed to and caught up in involvement in prayer, from the youngest believing child to the oldest saint. This is made possible simply by being utterly convinced of the normal and accessible place of prayer at the centre of everything and its accessibility to everyone. It is definitely not just for the super eloquent or articulate or theologically well-shaped. The earnest heartfelt cry of an uneducated person can move heaven to touch earth with a single sentence. Whatever else my goals in serving the local church are, I will have fallen short of New Testament priorities, if I rest content without trying my hardest to teach and model the establishing of a praying church culture.

Identity check

Another encouragement to see prayer as natural is the identity we have 'in Christ'; alive to God and joined in intimate union to God himself by the Holy Spirit. I am adopted as his son by grace through faith, simply due to the fact it gives him pleasure to have me as one of his dearly loved children. I might be worse than I think I am, and had more sin to be forgiven than I imagine, but I am also more accepted, valued, cared for and cherished by God than I can ever realise.

Prayer in such a relationship is not hard work when my new nature controls my flesh as it can and should. I want to tell God everything and cast all of my cares on him: I know he cares for me. I want all springs of joy and fulfilment to come from him. I want to enjoy all the blessings of life, not by making them into a god, but by giving thanks to God. He is not listening to my prayers in some disinterested frame of mind, giving occasional attention to me when I really go for it in prayer and get stirred up. He loves me and our fellowship is close and ongoing. Jesus, the second Adam, has made it possible for me to walk again with God in the cool of the evening and fellowship with him as the first Adam did before the fall.

Essence of prayer

Prayer is central to our walk with God, not supplementary. It's the engine of our relationship, not the wheels. Prayer is kindled by grace, not driven by need. God entreats us to make our requests known to him, but it's not 'petition'-driven. Prayer is spoken from walking alongside him, not from isolation, calling out to a distant friend for assistance, hoping somehow he can hear our cries for help. He is so close that he hears our heartbeat, perceives our thoughts and knows our words before they are vocalised.

Prayer takes many forms, including devotional and intercessory. It has many expressions: quiet, loud, solitary, corporate. Prayer is not defined in Scripture any more than the existence of God is proved. It's just assumed that God's people will pray to him. God cannot but be there. Man cannot but talk to him.

The Westminster shorter catechism says: 'Prayer is the offering up of our desires unto God for things agreeable to his will, in the name of Christ, with confession of our sins and thankful acknowledgement of his mercies'. [13]

This definition is not exhaustive, but we can see that prayer is born out of a sense of dependency on God. This is normal to the life lived by grace. From beginning to end we are dependent on the one who made us, saved us and will keep us.

Given this beautiful restored relationship, it's natural to pray and we are at our wisest in life when, even for a few moments in the course of a day, we withdraw from all that presses in on us and come before our Father in Heaven and gain perspective, bringing calmness and strength from him once more.

To grow in knowing God requires times when the only people in attendance at the meeting are us and God. Something within us wants to reach out and commune with him. It's part of being made in his image. Even those who do not know Christ, seek contact with a god or gods. This aspect of communion means that prayer is much more than just asking God for things. Prayer is the expression of hunger, thirst and longing for God which is then only satisfied through friendship with him, regardless of what things are received from that communion.

The more intimate we become with God, the more wise we become in prayer. Knowing silence, delay or an outcome different from that which we asked, are not the signs of an indifferent God, but the loving dealings of a Father, who is working out his will, in and through us. They provide us with opportunities to place our faith in his nature and character even when we do not see evidence of them at that moment. This is the essence of faith. Believing what God has said to be true even when there is no external corroboration of it being so.

Pour out your heart

To deny ourselves the joy and benefits of prayer is like having a bank account filled with thousands of pounds and never accessing it, but living instead on the meagre amounts our own efforts can secure.

We are given the most extraordinary encouragement about prayer in Philippians 4:6: *'Do not be anxious about anything, but in everything by prayer and supplication with thanksgiving let your requests be made known to God.'*

God does not ask us to ask him the things we think he wants us to ask about! Not the things that we think he will answer, nor the things that we can believe he will answer. Neither should we ask the things good Christians ought, so we can feel we have done it right. Rather, we are encouraged to make known our requests, even those which lie deep in our hearts that perhaps are unexpressed to anyone else. We are instructed to make continual and clear mention of our requests to our Father in Heaven; no restrictions, no limits on the number of times we ask, no 'off limits'. God wants to hear our hearts. He wants to know how you feel. Pour it out, unrestricted, unashamed and unprofessional!

Psalm 62:8: *'Trust in him at all times, O people; pour out your heart before him; God is a refuge for us.'*

Lamentations 2:19: *'Arise, cry out in the night, at the beginning of the night watches! Pour out your heart like water before the presence of the Lord!'*

God wants to hear the outpouring of our hearts and knows exactly how to respond. Knowing that he will answer brings peace beyond any comprehension or perspective on what we have prayed about. Peace descends on us like an all-encompassing presence of utter and complete rest. It is no longer our burden to carry for he has taken it upon himself to deal with.

1 Peter 5:7: *'Casting all your anxieties on him, because he cares for you'*

I am blessed to live in a house that directly overlooks a beach where I often walk and pray. I can remember times, when burdened with a worry or a care, picking up a big stone and saying 'Lord, this is my burden and care. I carry it around with me. You do not want me to do this, so I 'cast it' upon you'. I would then throw this huge rock into the mighty ocean and watch it disappear without trace. Its weight and largeness to me just got swallowed up in a vast pool of water! Casting my burdens on him means letting go of weights that are heavy and draining for me and throwing them into the ocean of God's promises and nature. They become his, not mine; a transfer has occurred. By his grace I can give him the things that weigh me down. 'He cares for me', so I throw my cares onto him in full confidence. He wants to take them and shield me from their harmful effects.

Dependency produces prayer

In 2 Corinthians 1:8-11 we read:

'For we do not want you to be ignorant, brothers, of the affliction we experienced in Asia. For we were so utterly burdened beyond our strength that we despaired of life itself. Indeed, we felt that we had received the sentence of death. But that was to make us rely not on ourselves but on God who raises the dead. He delivered us from such a deadly peril, and he will

deliver us. On him we have set our hope that he will deliver us
again. You also must help us by prayer, so that many will give
thanks on our behalf for the blessing granted us through the
prayers of many.'

Paul was totally in the will of God to be pioneering new church
plants in Asia. It was an open door for him. However, he wanted
his readers to know that even doing the right thing in the right
time and place, can bring pressures and challenges in large
measures. This is the reality of serving Christ.

Paul was 'burdened beyond his strength'. Such a phrase can
only mean he felt all his capacities to cope were exhausted.
He felt he could not manage any longer and despaired of life
itself. He felt under 'the sentence of death'. What was true for
Paul is true for any human facing extreme pressures, beyond
our ability to process and handle. Such pressure will not allow
us to stand still in our frame of mind or faith. We will either be
driven to God and pray or move towards despair and descend
the staircase of thoughts and feelings that only add to the
sense of hopelessness.

We are always dependent fully on God; even our next breath
is a gift. The fact we wake up again after our last night's
sleep is the providence of God. We are dependent, but do
not always feel it. The most effective Christians are those
who have taught their hearts to know and 'rely on God'. Paul
realised he faced pressures that God allowed; therefore he
would become more dependent on God.

Dependency is the currency of heaven. Simply put, the more
dependent on God we feel, the more effectively we will live
for him. The more he can do with us, the more he can entrust
to us. Thinking, acting and speaking from a dependent
perspective will change much of what we do and say. Also,
the more dependent we feel, the more we will pray and see

prayer as the only answer. Paul said in verse 11 *'you also must help us by prayer.'* He did not ask for anything else but prayer. He knew this was the prize commodity because dependency had been forced upon him.

Help for us to pray

We also have the huge encouragement of Romans 8:26: *'Likewise the Spirit helps us in our weakness. For we do not know what to pray for as we ought, but the Spirit himself intercedes for us with groanings too deep for words.'*

Even in pouring out our requests, we sense the imperfection of words not really conveying what we would want to say. A lack of power in prayer is felt as we get distracted and lose our train of thought. We do not pray as we ought to! Yet even these imperfect and incomplete attempts are taken up and presented by grace. The Holy Spirit transforms them into powerful pleadings that move the heart of God for our cause. Why would we not pray and try to pray and keep trying to pray all through our lives when such help is at hand?

Building a prayer life is like running a marathon to win a prize. Sometimes we feel lightness in our feet and we fairly sprint along. At other times our feet feel like lead, but then someone comes along and carries us for a bit until our tired limbs find fresh energy. God is committed to helping us run the race of prayer and he helps us at every turn. I go through seasons where prayer has more energy to it than at others. I have learned not to fret over such variances, but to keep in fellowship with the Lord by faith and wait for him to renew and restore me.

Weak prayers and wasted time

God even hears and responds to my seemingly bad or weak prayers. I live in unbroken communion with him and do not have to wait for the elevator to take me up to heavenly places. He has already raised me up and seated me there with Christ. There is no 'down' button any more.

The image of God, routinely walking in the cool of the Garden of Eden at evening time looking to fellowship with Adam is how it is with us. Our relationship restored with God through Christ recaptures the ease that flowed out of the deep fellowship in Eden prior to the fall. Our second Adam has opened the way for such communion again to flow in every moment of each day. In such context, a natural desire and outflow to our relationship should be extended communion and ever-increasing depth of fellowship with God.

In my seemingly sometimes wasted time with God, when I am dull of mind and slow of speech, I am able to say to him, 'Lord this is not very good prayer today but I am here with you'. That in itself redeems the moment; God likes me wasting time with him. It is not an appointment but a companionship of ever deepening intimacy and unhurried communion.

Keep going

Colossians 4:2-4: *'Continue steadfastly in prayer, being watchful in it with thanksgiving. At the same time, pray also for us, that God may open to us a door for the word, to declare the mystery of Christ, on account of which I am in prison— that I may make it clear, which is how I ought to speak.'*

To Paul's mind there is an assumption that prayer would be a regular feature of Christian living. The encouragement is not to start, but to continue. Such persistence and focus in prayer is for Paul the key to his emerging strategy. 'That God may open a door for us'. Paul does not sit down with a flip chart, marker pen and a room full of 'bright young men' and ask for help creating a five year plan! Rather, he prays and wants others to pray, so God will make the next part of the strategy clear by opening doors that then are obvious and can be walked through. This is so helpful to us in life as when we walk through a door God has so obviously opened, it gives us faith to continue.

Even if we encounter difficulty, opposition and set-back as we progress, we can rightly and confidently say to God: 'you said!' Starting a ministry, business, or fresh church plant without the certainty that God is the originator is a frightening place to be when problems occur. Prayer often involves going back to God with promises and saying: 'Lord, you said'. This gives confidence and we can say: 'Lord I am doing to the best of my knowledge what you said to do. Now Lord you will need to make this work as I cannot on my own. I will do what you have told me, please Lord now do what you have said'.

Prayer that is 'watchful' and 'thankful' in an ongoing way will help create the environment, both in church life and personally, where God finds it easy to do what he desires to do. This is the oil that helps the wheels of Heaven's purposes to go round.

We achieve by praying more and doing less. In fact, the more we face increased pressure, the more we must make persistent, prevailing prayer our very heartbeat. Prayer works. God is sovereign over all things: events, people, places and history. He is Alpha and Omega, who knows the beginning and the end and holds them in his hands. They are both present-time to him who dwells outside of time, or space, or any other such constrict. Yet in his sovereignty he has chosen to bring about his purposes by responding to the prayers of his people throughout the generations. For his own unfathomable reasons, he has chosen to outwork his purposes in tandem with our prevailing engagement in prayer.

Prayer is therefore not an added extra to boost our relationship with God. Rather, it's the means of fleshing out in reality the purposes of God on the earth. It is entirely appropriate to carry a sense of responsibility with regard to prayer. Our prayers can affect the destiny and blessing of many.

Grace in delays

Sometimes, greater depths in God occur in the lives of those who have to pray the longest. These people face a seemingly solid brass heaven where no indication of an answer is apparent. Sometimes God's answer to our prayers is silence because there are things that cannot be achieved in any other way. We do not live in a world used to delay. Current Christian culture is moving more and more towards expecting and anticipating the immediate in matters relating to the purposes of God. This is simply not biblical. Delay and patience are features of the lives and journeys of many of those in Scripture, used by God. I have sometimes heard 'bright' and seemingly 'flourishing' leaders say things in team meetings like 'we can do this', or 'look at the potential of leadership in this room'. I cannot find one single instance in the Bible where anyone used by God spoke in such a way. Quite the opposite is true. We simply cannot put our agenda on God and predict the timescale.

Persistent, unwearied and unswerving confidence in God's willingness and love towards us must be developed. We need to be convinced that God not only hears, but rewards with answers. Why sometimes does he delay or withhold what we have asked for, or apparently refuse our deepest longings? Such questions can only be answered in the sure and certain resting place of God's nature and character, which is nothing but love, kindness, compassion and wisdom towards those whom he has redeemed. The only reason God would say 'no' to something is ultimately to say 'yes' to something better for us. We can't always see this, but it's always true.

To trust him when we cannot see his plan in what is happening to us; to accept his will when it seems so strange and goes against our deepest longings; to talk to him when he only seems to listen and never reply or act or reassure; to place all our confidence in him, even when it looks like he would almost kill us: that is the behaviour of those who know him best.

Many have found themselves praying about something for long years. How do we make sense of what is happening through such dark and silent times? Perhaps it can be likened to firing an arrow from a bow. When drawn back a little way, the ultimate distance, effect and power of the fired arrow is small. However, when the bow is drawn back to its long, maximum stretch with great effort and dedication, it causes a release of force greater than that which a human can exert. Prayer under these circumstances can release such a punch as to tear through armour and pierce the heart of the enemy of our souls.

God is not counting our quantity of prayers, nor assessing their style, poetry, logic or doctrine. He is essentially looking for men and women who will not let go of him until they are assured about who he is and what he has promised. They will not cease until their prayers come to pass and he blesses them in accordance with his promises. They draw the bow back confident of ultimately gaining maximum flight and punch in the things God has promised.

How to develop your personal prayer life

I am somewhat reluctant to talk technique as the Bible does not seem to do so. God presumably knows that in giving the bare minimum of essential structure, we can find our way. 'Seek and you will find', he says. However, as young believers we do not automatically know how to construct a prayer life. Hence the disciples asking Jesus 'teach us how to pray'. Building a grace-filled routine is important to living a life of

grace and growing in God. The disciples asked Jesus how to
pray because they were stimulated to develop communion
with the Father by what they saw Jesus had. They were rightly
jealous for it. They were not after a set of religious rules to
keep God happy, but a framework to facilitate a relationship.
We get married to enjoy the relationship, not to have the
wedding certificate!

Developing a habit of prayer

Apparently research shows that to a habit takes on average
28 days make or break. Spending time with God each day,
ideally before with anyone else, is a good habit to form. Prayer
benefits from building-in set times, routines and locations in
our lifestyle so as to avoid a chaotic approach to something
so important. However, it is also hugely important to bear
in mind that we are to live life in constant communion with
God throughout the normal activities of daily life. Christians
in the middle-ages often referred to this as the 'practice of
the presence of God'. This delightful concept was aimed at
showing us that life could be permeated by awareness of
the presence of God in even the most routine and menial of
tasks. Doing all to the glory of God and in companionship and
communion with him, was not only possible but desirable.
Believing God is always 'near' is the key to developing such
communion. We truly do not go to church and meet God, or
spend time in prayer only to go on our way in life awaiting the
next encounter. He is with us all the time.

How often to pray?

The Bible has 'Evening' psalms (prayers) to reflect on God at
the end of a day's work. For example, Psalm 4:8: *'In peace I will
both lie down and sleep; for you alone O Lord make me dwell in
safety'.* There are also, 'Morning' psalms such as Psalm 5:3:
'O Lord in the morning, you hear my voice'. Mark 1:35 reveals

that Jesus took regular time early in the morning to be with his Father. We find Daniel prayed three times a day while 1 Thessalonians 5:17 encourages us to develop a lifestyle of constant communion with God, to 'pray without ceasing'. These verses and others indicate that prayer should become a well-developed habit that punctuates all of life. In short, we are to pray at all times, on all occasions and combine this with the development of our own regular 'prayer times'.

Where to pray?

Under the Old Covenant certain places, individuals and external practices were more acceptable in prayer than others at various times. The New Covenant removes all of this. All who are in Christ can now pray wherever and whenever they want. We can now come boldly with confidence to God in prayer, assured of a welcome into his presence at any time in any place (Hebrews 4:16).

In Mark 1:35 we see that Jesus went alone to pray where he would not be disturbed. Matthew 6:6 indicates a private location is helpful to us where we will not be disturbed unduly. So whether indoors or outside, we need somewhere to be alone with God, free from distractions but perhaps somewhere visually conducive.

The style of prayer

We can speak normally and pray in tongues. We can pray back to God truths and promises from portions of scripture; sing a prayer, quietly or noisily, even silently. It should be with an attitude of passion as we read in Hebrews 5:7: *'Jesus offered up prayers… with loud cries and tears… He was heard because of his reverence'.*

We should talk and listen; give thanks, intercede, lament, adore and request. We can stand, sit, kneel and walk. We may lift our hands and faces to heaven; crouch with head between our knees and lie prostrate on the ground.

There are many books explaining how we can structure our prayer life in terms of what we pray for and when. After many experiments and not surprisingly, I have found that the answer Jesus gave to his disciples is in fact the best advice on how to pray. It can be framed in a whole range of styles according to the moment.

The 'Lord's Prayer' as it has become known is not a chant to be repeated. Neither is it a straightjacket that has to be put on every time we pray. It's a framework that, if followed, ensures we focus with the right emphasis on the things that God wants us to. For example, beginning with 'Father' as our starting point and only later focusing our attention on 'forgive us our sins', avoids the scenario whereby our failures receive a higher profile than God himself does. Sin needs to be confessed and brought to God, but according to Jesus, is not the place to start. Using the Lord's prayer model as a structure for your regular devotional life, will help you relate well to God in prayer. This is true whether you have five minutes or a whole day to pray!

From combining the text in Matthew 6:9-13 and Luke 11:2-4 where the Lord's Prayer is located, our pattern of prayer should flow as follows:

Father
We begin our prayer time by starting with the basis of our relationship with God. We come to him firstly as Father. During this section remind yourself of this; settle the matter in your heart; 'my Father'. Approach him from this relational and intimate standing. In prayer we are not talking to an unknown God but in communion with 'the Father'. Knowing we come to our 'Father' in Heaven should then remove all hesitancy or uncertainty about what kind of a reception we will receive.

Hallowed be your name

When we read the Psalms and see the expansive nature of prayer contained in them, it's clear that knowledge of God's nature and character form the basis for effective prayer. The psalmist knew the God he was seeking: everlasting, almighty, Lord of Hosts. Having a clear view of who God is enables us to come boldly and with confidence. It also enables our worship of him to be in 'truth' as we see him for who he is.

In this section try focusing on just one of the aspects of God's character or attributes, bringing worship and thanksgiving and reverence to him for this aspect of who he is. In this way, a deeper, more thorough knowledge of who God is in all his fullness can be explored and enjoyed

Your Kingdom come

Here you can bring situations to God that you feel you want to bring to his attention: prayer for other people, your church, your family, in fact anything where the rule of God is required. Ask for his kingdom activity to break in and energize these aspects of your life.

Your will be done

Ask God for his guidance in particular situations here so that things proceed the way 'his will' would desire. Again all manner of things can come under this heading.

Give us this day our daily bread

In this section you can bring the needs of yourself and your family; daily health, strength, protection and material provision. Be specific about needs, whether small or large, God does care about the details of our lives; Proverbs 30:8-9 shows the rightness and importance of praying for provision.

Forgive us our sins for we also forgive everyone who sins against us

Again be specific; ask God if there is anything he sees in you that needs correcting. I have found asking God this question often leads to him telling me things I had forgotten about or was not even aware of. The Holy Spirit will often speak to your conscience concerning confession. During this time, make sure that if you have any wrong attitudes towards others for what they have done, forgive and release them. This goes in hand with our request for personal cleansing. If you cannot think of anything to confess, then don't confess at all. It is possible to have not sinned since you last prayed!

Lead us not into temptation but deliver us from the evil one

It is important to pray that God will protect us from the schemes and traps of the enemy. We all need to take care that we don't fall, especially if we are feeling confident. An attitude of dependence on God's ongoing guaranteed protection is a healthy perspective on life. Remember that greater is he that is in us, than he that is in the world. However, we do have an enemy who is powerful and has plans and who will wait for an opportune time. To pray, 'deliver us from him', is therefore sound advice!

For yours is the Kingdom for ever and ever… Amen!

End your prayer time by reminding yourself that he is able to do more than all you ask or think. It is his kingdom that rules and it is eternal and unchanging.

12 *Grace to grow in community*

We are made in God's image as human beings. Even with the effects of the fall, we still in glimpses reflect the glory of God. God is revealed to us in Scripture as Father, Son and Holy Spirit. We use the word 'Trinity' to describe this three and yet one essential essence of God.

God exists in community. He told Adam that it was not good for him to be alone. Eve was made to complete his reflection of the image of God. Mankind reflects the glory of God therefore, only when expressed in community. God has always wanted a people, not a collection of individuals. Ephesians 3:9-10 tells us God's plan was:

'To bring to light for everyone what is the plan of the mystery hidden for ages in God who created all things, so that through the church the manifold wisdom of God might now be made known'

God displays his glory through the visible church on the earth. The church is essentially a noun not a verb. We do not 'do' church, rather as his people we 'are' church. Local expressions in every nation, people group and culture expressing his image and glory in redeemed humanity.

Disillusioned with church

A troubling trend in recent years has been observed. Numbers of Christians no longer consider themselves part of a local church. Many do not see this as necessary or even desirable, to live out their Christian profession. Some people have been hurt through church, suffering abuses of authority and wrong teaching. There have been disputes and falling out with other people, painful issues and dashed hopes.

Sadly, this catalogue of common occurrences has caused many people to be very wary of being part of a local church. It's easy to understand why someone would think twice about joining another church if they have already been hurt by one community of God's people. They thought they were safe from these things. Why take the risk of it happening again?

Although understandable, such fears are unhelpful as when it works it is quite magnificent. God's plan is for marriage between a man and woman. Yet we all know of sad situations where marriage has not worked out. Do we then conclude, 'let's find an alternative arrangement as marriage no longer works?' God has purposed that marriage reflects his glory in the earth in how men and woman live together. God has also equally purposed for his church to reflect his glory in the world. On these things God's opinion has not changed.

Only with the grace of God can a marriage function well. Only with the grace of God can a church function well. This is God's intention. We need his grace and it is available. Glory flows to God in a marriage or church without issues, where life is wonderful. But surely the glory of God is seen most visibly where people come through against many odds. They live magnificent lives of attractive quality and inspirational character under the mighty gracious hand of God as they find themselves living dependently in an ongoing way. Surely this is the arena where grace is seen and demonstrated as being quite sufficient for our every need.

How magnificent is a marriage that has found grace to thrive and flourish through many years! Or to see a church that is thriving in its local community. Surely these are most excellent things to behold. Do not allow what has gone bad to rob you of what can be so good!

Diluted church

Furthermore the advent of 'God' TV channels and the internet means that we can now experience something of church at the touch of a button. Then, when we no longer want to listen or are bored, we can move on to the next thing to fulfill our appetites. This can be done without at any time enduring the perceived inconvenience and irritation of interaction with people whom we might not even like. No wonder it appeals to the western individualistic consumer: all gain no pain!

Others are experimenting with so called new ways of doing church: 'liquid church', 'emergent church' and 'experimental church'. But any expression of church that moves away from a gathered local community of redeemed individuals, led by God's appointed leadership and built on apostolic doctrine and practice, is less than New Testament church. We are selling ourselves short and depriving God of something he has had on his heart to do through many centuries prior to Christ.

The answer to church being a bad experience is not to abandon it but to build it well. Many people are glad to belong to their local church. They are loved, taught well and their gifts are used to bless others. Relationships and community is genuine and mission catches them up into something beyond their own little world and gives them a perspective on God's bigger picture.

Grace lived out in community

Quite recently I have attended a few Christian weddings and been struck by just how much that Christians really do know how to party and enjoy themselves without sinning. I have witnessed those who are not Christians and not from a church community at all, being completely outshone on the dance floor by effusive explosions of life in all its fullness. I've noted work-friends and family of bride and groom, trying to look cool in what they see as 'their' environment. As the disco lights flash, they prepare to display their prowess, only to be totally upstaged by carefree, happy Christians. I observe that most people don't know what to do with this! Why should we not rejoice in the things in life that are good and give us joy? This is part of the redemption of life, that we can celebrate the good things in life and do it without sin.

We are told in Scripture to rejoice with those that rejoice and to weep with those that weep. As a church community grows, so both of these things are more frequently happening side by side. Life is full of both happy and sad events. Christian weddings and funerals show how grace flows in happy and sad times to and through God's people. Occasions of deep hope and emotions, shared joy and sorrow, a sense of family and grieving but not without hope, quite simply are amongst the most profound emotional human interactions possible. If we remove church, we rob ourselves of God's gracious provision to our needs and that of others. We rob God of his glory in the world, of his wisdom being demonstrated through life's happy and sad periods.

One city in Europe has such an isolated and individualistic culture, that if you had more than 12 people attending your funeral, you would be considered a very popular person. How sad is that? The church is intended to be a community where all of life is shared, not superficially but a deep and powerful way

Grace for people

Galatians 6 speaks of the fruit of the Holy Spirit in our lives as being: love, joy, peace, patience, kindness and long-suffering. We might feel we are very patient but only in church community can this claim be validated. How can we be patient unless we have someone to be patient with? How can we be kind unless we have someone to be kind to? How can we love unless we have someone to love?

The manner in which people relate to each other, argue and mishandle relating together is the stuff of spiritual growth. Local church community shapes us so we learn to listen to each other, understand different perspectives and learn how to treat people more appropriately. The Bible encourages us to realise that the church is like a body and though the foot might be very different from the eye, both need and learn from each other's differences. We simply cannot grow as Christians without being part of God's community which is the local church - founded well, led well, taught well, full of word and Spirit and grace lived out. Find one that most looks like the New Testament if you're not in one, and join it!

We may sing songs about giving all to Jesus and seeking to serve his purposes in sacrificial love. The reality is his purposes are for the local church to thrive and flourish throughout the world. The local church has always been 'Plan A' for reaching the world and is the prime context for maturing God's people. Our sacrificial willingness must be grounded in working out our calling. This happens by serving those around us in the local church and by reaching the unsaved community we live in through the church.

Church community provides us with the life-setting to become more like Christ and to live out the grace of God that is working in us. There are similar challenges in the work place to be Christ-like, but we do not withdraw from the world of work because people are difficult to get along with. Yet for some reason we seem to expect that church should not present us with any relational challenges and if there are some, it is somehow acceptable to withdraw. Christians are works in progress and we need grace with each other.

It takes a lot to handle gossip and the divisive person who spreads untruths about you round your friends. It's difficult to handle being ignored or left out by the person you have given yourself to helping and including when they were in need. The Bible anticipates we will need help in our relationships with those in the world and those in the church. Explicit instructions are given on how to handle ourselves when faced with relationships that are not going the way we had hoped.

So let us resist the tempted to abandon local Church life because of being hurt by other people in the same community. Forgiveness, character and maturity are required.

Grace to change through local church life

Most of us wish we were different in many ways. Not so noisy, not so shy, not so negative, not so sarcastic or cynical. Some of the character traits we have that are not Christ-like, we can do something about. However, some aspects of our personality can be either good or bad depending on how we manage them; they make us are who we are and are not going to change. Some of us are sanguine and essentially fun-loving, optimistic, spontaneous types; some are more choleric, comfortable with tasks and achievements. Varieties of personality are aspects of our 'flesh', fallen and as yet not redeemed, and therefore subject to appetites and influences which can make them sinful and require adjustment. Psalm 139:23-24 says:

'Search me, O God, and know my heart! Try me and know my thoughts! And see if there be any grievous way in me, and lead me in the way everlasting!'

This encourages us to see how change and adjustment in the Christian life should work. We should live an open accountable life to God with an attitude that says: 'Lord if there is anything in my life requiring adjustment, that is not bringing you pleasure or joy when you look at how I am in this matter, please tell me'. We then leave the initiative with God rather than go digging around trying to find things. The Devil will only too happily lend a hand in the search and help you recall what had been forgotten. This prayer is not asking that we be reminded of faults now forgiven. Rather, the plea is to reveal where ongoing issues remain that hinder God's glory and power from flowing fully in particular areas of life.

If God then shows us something, our attitude should be adjusted; we must change how we think and act. Ongoing confession of sins already forgiven does nothing to please God or help us. It calls into question our belief in his promises and restricts us from hearing his voice into the issues he sees of importance. So how does God show us areas that need adjustment? Mostly it comes about through our ongoing interactions with people. Growth in Christ-likeness is not a solo activity; it's worked out in community church life.

Grace to be accountable

Some discipleship has gone wrong and terms like 'heavy shepherding' have arisen when it is sensed leaders are speaking into areas of people's lives not required or encouraged by Scripture. Quite frankly, what colour you paint your kitchen or where you go on holiday is not the business of church leaders. We are not to create dependent people, unable to make wise mature decisions. Rather, the aim is for all to reach maturity so that our lives are pleasing to the Lord in how we conduct ourselves in all regards.

This does not mean we are to be independent, but to be those who recognise the need for our brothers and sisters in Christ. Accountability is the valuing of the contribution others make to our progress in Christ-likeness. This in turn makes a person eager, where appropriate, to give a reckoning/ explanation for their actions, recognizing that they do not have all the resources they need to successfully navigate life's course on their own. Those who recognise God's provision of others for their wellbeing will have no problems being accountable. Accountability is different from being answerable. Being answerable involves a willingness to answer questions, if and when asked. Accountability means, a willing opening up of yourself, without having to be asked, by those Godly and mature Christians you have come to trust.

Many people shrink from 'accountability' as it sounds like lack of freedom. But the reality is that we are all accountable in a variety of ways.

To God Hebrews 4:13:

'And no creature is hidden from his sight, but all are naked and exposed to the eyes of him to whom we must give account'.

We will one day give an account for our lives.

To each other Ephesians 5:21:

'Submitting to one another out of reverence for Christ'.

There is no hierarchy in church life; we all need to have an attitude of mutual respect and honour for each other, coupled with a willingness to receive from each other. We are also accountable to civil authorities as it is God who has placed them in the positions they are in. We cannot get away from the fact that accountability is part of being human.

Grace to be helped by others

There are considerable benefits to being accountable. We are less likely to have blind spots or to make the same silly mistakes if we have trusted friends who help us see the vulnerable areas. We have examples in the Bible. Samuel helped Saul understand himself better, Jonathan helped David, and Paul confronted Peter when he started to get into error. We need people like this.

Mature advisors can help us avoid what to them are obvious traps. We naturally see everything in life one way – our way.

If, however, we open up and talk about our lives to a spiritually mature person, he may see things we do not. He may hear us talking and observe a potential trap or issue that we may not have realised was there.

Prov13: 10: *'Pride breeds only quarrels, but wisdom is found in those who take advice.'*

With the counsel of a friend or friends, we are more likely to become aware of all the aspects of a situation; to gain depth and perspective, and find another scenario or possible solution which by ourselves we may have missed.

Prov27: 17: *'As iron sharpens iron, so one man sharpens another.'*

As we make ourselves accountable and appropriately vulnerable to others, we are less likely to fool and excuse ourselves about following the wrong desires of our heart. In this way, being accountable reduces the risk of sinning. How? As we discuss a situation with someone, he may take a risk and point out things we are choosing to ignore or those things we don't wish to hear. In these ways he may actually wound us, but we need to keep in mind this is for our own good.

Prov27: 6: *'The kisses of an enemy may be profuse, but faithful are the wounds of a friend.'*

With accountability we are more likely to be helped in correcting otherwise ingrained habits and lifestyle issues that need correction. Research has shown that it takes 28 days to form or break a habit. Someone to stand with us in these areas can provide extra incentive and motivation. It can end up being very practical: health issues such as drinking, being under- or over-weight, and smoking; spiritual issues such as time with God, reading the Bible; lifestyle issues such as laziness, serving God, being a good parent, husband or wife, managing money better. The list is endless.

Grace to relate rightly to people

I guess most people who have been Christians for any length of time will at some point have been hurt by other Christians, sometimes very deeply. As we reflect on such things it's all too easy to pull up the draw bridge and conclude: 'I will never get close to anyone ever again as I do not want to risk that re-occurring'.

This response, whilst completely understandable, is never going to produce good results. What it reveals is that we have not as yet worked through the hurt nor been able to place our faith in Christ for all aspects of our lives.

Jesus was repeatedly let down, even by those closest to him. The apostle Paul commented in 2 Timothy 1:15: 'you know that everyone in the province of Asia has deserted me'. He had good reason for deciding in the future: 'I will do it alone, thanks'.

We have to come to the place of laying down self-protection where it would compromise the formation of other deep and God-honouring relationships. There are others who need us to be deeply relational and not closed books of suspicion. It communicates non-verbally when someone is edgy in relationships. At worst, rejection can take root and we become so suspicious of all kindness expressed towards us that we react sometimes subconsciously to reject the person and hurt them so they cannot hurt us first.

Grace must be allowed to dig down deep into our hearts and uproot any such thing. Jesus was spoken against, jeered at and carried the utmost rejection so that we do not have to. He ministers by his grace into rejection and breaks its ugly cycle, so we are free to trust and take risks in relationships again, free in his grace.

We have to become willing to be accountable and take the risks involved in building deep relationships of trust with God's people. Lack of willingness to do this is often the reason why people fail to change and grow in grace. Those most likely to grow in God are those who look to be accountable and build relationships with people.

Some people are not trustworthy as they have not matured enough themselves. We are to be discerning about who we relate to and how. It is important to find good-hearted brothers and sisters in Christ, who are for us and there to genuinely help. The truth spoken may be challenging to hear but is a kindness to us. If we are in relationships with people full of the Holy Spirit and exhibiting his fruit in their lives, then with just a few words, much can be affected in us for good. I would never have wanted to deny myself the privilege of being shaped and moulded by some of the great men and women of God it has been my utmost privilege to know. To spend an hour with them and listen to their wisdom; to simply enjoy watching how they do life, is in itself a source of grace to me.

Grace to make the circle bigger

A church should always be growing bigger and maturing in Christ-likeness. Quality and quantity are not enemies. As a local church community of God's people seek to live out the Christian life, those outside the church should be attracted by what is on display.

John 13:35: *'By this all men will know that you are my disciples, if you love one another.'*

People are not won merely by words; they are convinced of the authenticity of our words when they see them lived out in reality. We are encouraged to live out life not in hidden obscurity but as a lamp on a stand. This does not mean brash display but open visible manifestation of Christ-likeness through his Church.

We are all called to reach people with the gospel. For some this is best done through proclamation, for others it is through friendship and more interpersonal gifting. The grace of God when it has really taken root in a local church will inevitably produce outward looking people who are less and less taken up with thoughts about themselves and their well-being or personal happiness. Instead they will instinctively, through the washing of the grace of God, become selfless people always looking to include the lost, the hurt and the broken; the friendless, the socially challenged and the marginalised; all races, all social sectors, the rich and poor. Grace lived out reaches out. This is not a program, it is a culture.

My observation is that the more people become comfortable in their identity in Christ and comfortable in who they are in relation to others, the more the local church community exudes peace, calm, grace and acceptance and becomes hugely attractive to be amongst. Those who do not as yet believe should find us a wonderful people to be with. Nothing to prove; nothing to be afraid of; people secure in Christ and what it means to believe in him!

13 *Grace to give and receive*

Giving and grace are linked. Grace changes all the perspectives we once had, some instantly and some gradually. It is not just about money, it is about a changed attitude to giving and receiving.

Money, money, money

Grace does not mean we live life in some ad hoc undisciplined way, deciding on a whim what we will or will not do for God. Grace strengthens and energizes us, giving us a disciplined focus and a thankful heart that changes selfish motivation into motivation for his glory.

Giving of our finances is one example. I think it was John Wesley who said, 'If God touches a man's heart he will touch his wallet also'. Abraham was one of the first people in Scripture to show us a grace-motivated response of worship that included monetary giving to God.

Genesis 14:20: *'And Abram gave him a tenth of everything'.*

Whoever the receiver Melchizedek in verse 18 was, it is not relevant to our point. The issue is Abraham was thankful to God for his presence, mercy and intervention in his life and his giving was a response of worship and thankfulness to God.

This example of proportional grace-motivated giving was before the Law, which then standardised the tithe and the occasions on which varying amounts of giving was tithed. Later in the New Testament, rather than discarding the principle of proportional giving, Jesus actually encouraged it as long as it was with a grace-filled attitude, which embraced more significant perspectives like justice and mercy rather than a purely religious motive.

Matthew 23:23: *'Woe to you, scribes and Pharisees, hypocrites! For you tithe mint and dill and cumin, and have neglected the weightier matters of the law: justice and mercy and faithfulness. These you ought to have done, without neglecting the others.'*

In 1 Corinthians 16:2 The New Testament church was encouraged to have a regular proportional attitude to giving:

'On the first day of every week, each one of you should set aside a sum of money in keeping with his income, saving it up, so that when I come no collections will have to be made.'

Grace and discipline are not enemies; they serve each other if handled rightly. From scriptural encouragement it would seem that each Christian who earns money should give at least 10% of their earnings to the local church they are part of. God in his wisdom planned it this way and it is not only honouring to God and part of our true worship, it is the economy of God for his local church.

For example, supposing a new church is being started in a locality and has 40 wage earners. By the time it launches publicly, using this principle of 10%, enough finance would be available for a leader to put initial plans into action. As the church then continues to grow and other wage earners join, budgeting for expansion becomes possible. The economy of the church and its financial capacity is increased, thus providing the resources for the church to move forward into further stages of ministry. This is how the grace and discipline of giving helps to serve the advancement of the Gospel.

Heart motivation

All giving should be done with a heart touched and living in the good of grace. As 2 Corinthians 9:7 says:

'Each man should give what he has decided in his heart to give, not reluctantly or under compulsion, for God loves a cheerful giver.'

A good barometer of how we are doing in our relationship with God is how we feel about giving our finances. None of us ever has enough money. We all occasionally say to ourselves, 'If I only had another £500, all would be so much easier.' These are the times when it is vital to reflect on where our true treasure lies.

We are lonely passing through this world and in reality it is outwardly a very unfair place. Some of us will go through life quite well off, with good holidays, fine hotels and restaurants. We have good health, a nice spacious house and a decent job. Others meanwhile struggle from cradle to grave. The further away from the western-developed world, the more this is the case. We may feel fed up because our Spanish holiday has not materialised or been cancelled; but others are simply grateful for clean drinking water today, even if a two mile walk was involved!

Western media and popular culture endlessly seeks to create in our minds a mirage of how life should be for everyone. Such illusion can subtly and dangerously distort a Christian's expectations and aspirations. We may pray 'give us our daily bread' in order to gain health, wealth and prosperity and see the Cross as bringing the right to instant and total removal of all pain and suffering.

Such distortion produces an attitude that views our giving of money, time, gifts and prayers as an investment into a Kingdom bank from which we expect a high yield in this life. However, praying 'your kingdom come' should not be done selfishly to gain 'reward tokens' but with a heart that really does long for God's rule to be established.

Jesus came to defeat the works of the evil one. The Kingdom has come but not yet fully: it has grown and will continue to grow and extend. Jesus healed the sick, yet at present people still become sick. He raised Lazarus from the dead yet he must have died again (unless anyone knows where he is). Jesus stilled storms yet we have had many natural disasters since and he defeated death yet we are all dying! He brought in the kingdom, but he also told us to pray 'your kingdom come.'

Giving should flow as the response of a heart touched by grace. It is a practical demonstration of our love and commitment to him and is not for us to get anything out of. True enough, if I give my money then I may benefit from the principle *'that whoever sows generously will reap generously.'* (2 Cor 9:6). However this is a by-product not a motivation for giving.

Generous church

Church culture should reflect the heart of God. Not only does he look after us, but also those who at present hate him! Now that is grace indeed! *'For he makes his sun rise on the evil and on the good and sends rain on the just and on the unjust.'* (Matthew 5:45)

Church should have a culture of generosity. I hate seeing church buildings or facilities with second-hand furniture or drab décor. I get the impression of someone saying: "it is no longer good enough for my house, but the church can have it!" If church buildings look drab and out-dated, it shows a culture in the people of the church that is not grace-based. We should not 'live in a palace but worship in a pig sty'.

Some would then respond that many churches have so invested in their facilities that the needs of people have been neglected. Surely then, the answer must be that we employ, service and facilitate the use of church facilities that suit the culture we are seeking to serve. Anything that detracts from the message through either being overstated or shabby must be avoided. What is suitable in a developing country may well not be appropriate in a developed one and vice versa.

How we treat those whose livelihood is derived from serving in the local church is also an area when grace in generosity should be evident, especially leadership.

*'Let the elders who rule well be considered worthy of double
honour, especially those who labour in preaching and teaching'.*
For the Scripture says, *'You shall not muzzle an ox when it
treads out the grain,'* and, *'The labourer deserves his wages.'*
(1 Timothy 5:17-19)

A leader who is doing a good job in his role and function
should not have to minister in a culture of 'God will keep him
humble and we will keep him poor!' The benefits of a senior
team and wise trustees or deacons who can make corporate
decisions on all these matters are clear to see. But it goes
beyond issues of pay. It should affect the quality of welcome
we give people, the quality of our publicity and newsletters,
the refreshments, the décor and the willingness of the church
to serve people in the community who are so broken and
have such great needs that they might never be in a position
to give more than they receive.

Generosity means waiting to hear what someone wants to
say before you give your opinion. It means looking down
physically at the little people (children) and giving attention
to them. We should never get to the point where the system
stops serving the people. Generosity means multiplying an
army of people who give and give again to those who come
into contact with the church. They may have needs that they
would find hard to walk through alone. Only a grace-taught
community does these things without thinking! It is in their
DNA and goes way beyond the use of money.

Grace to receive

Have you ever had someone give you something purely
because they wanted to bless you? Perhaps they don't have
much themselves, but suddenly they're thrusting an envelope
into your hand or placing a parcel of food on your doorstep!
Hard isn't it? When faced with such kindness, some people

feel the need to respond with a level of thankfulness that will somehow pay for the gesture and make them more deserving of receiving it.

Hopefully however, the giver is not looking for payment. The kindness flows from a heavenly source, from God who gave his son just because he loved us. He only wanted to bless you and they only wanted to do likewise, albeit in a much lesser way. We are unconditioned to such gestures and wonder what the catch is. True enough sometimes when people do give us things, there is a catch, but not always. Grace when known and grasped frees us from all self-justification. It does this as we see we can never pay back or deserve what we have been given.

Our Father, who freely gives, is not vulnerable to sudden changes of perspective on us that would cause any change of heart in his motivation to give to us at all. We are useless in making any contribution to our cause being a valid one. All we can do is be thankful, enjoy and use the gift for the purpose for which it was given.

Church is a most wonderful place and I have had the privilege of being on a journey with a great local church for many years now. We still have many mountain peaks to climb and demonstrations of his glory to see happen amongst us.

As yet I have still to see anywhere in the West, something of the overspill of grace captured by the early church in the remarkable scenes witnessed in Acts. Scenes of care and generosity to each other as the need arose.

'And they were selling their possessions and belongings and distributing the proceeds to all, as any had need.' (Acts 2:45)

Attempts have been made to systematize this kind of community quality, but in truth only grace can produce it, systems cannot.

14 *A grace-filled life*

A book full of principles and theological reflections can help objectively to cast a firm anchor down into the sea of experience and hold a person steady through all kinds of winds and waves. Further encouragement might also be found from some personal reflections on how grace has practically appeared and helped me during a variety of situations and seasons in life.

Understanding and walking

All of the discoveries I have made can be traced to a principle found throughout the Bible. One such example of it is articulated in Colossians 1:9-10 where it says:

'And so, from the day we heard, we have not ceased to pray for you, asking that you may be filled with the knowledge of his will in all spiritual wisdom and understanding, so as to walk in a manner worthy of the Lord, fully pleasing to him, bearing fruit in every good work and increasing in the knowledge of God.'

Note in these verses the link between 'understanding' and 'walking'. We do not just drift into pleasing God and it certainly isn't a case of 'let go and let God'! Our hearts and minds need educating and instructing in the ways of grace. We find throughout the process that the Holy Spirit gives us grace to apply what we have seen and believed by faith from the revelation in Scripture.

We need God to help and that is what he does. Life's entire course is used to train and mature us to be more pleasing and fruitful to him. The providential interventions of God go far beyond our ability to put two and two together and understand what he was doing in any given situation. There is a master plan of wisdom unfolding that causes even angels to cry 'Glory to God'; just as when they saw the master plan of salvation unfolding in history. Who could have foreseen such wisdom?

Grace to calm my heart

I remember hearing the gospel preached clearly at the age of 17 by the newly arrived pastor of the church I attended. His blend of personal warmth and lucid communication style, all wrapped up in the anointing of the Holy Spirit on his life was a powerful combination. I was deeply convicted of my guilt and shame before God, the destiny of Hell if not saved and my consequent need of a saviour.

At the end of the sermon, he issued an invitation to anyone who wanted to respond to join him at the front. Mostly through embarrassment and self-consciousness, my feet stayed firmly rooted to the spot. But in my heart I was 'nailed' and so I turned to Christ where I was, and prayed some sort of sinner's prayer.

My problems following this initial confrontation with the truth, centred around being unsure whether my feeble - and perhaps poorly worded - prayer of acceptance of Christ had worked or not. For a start, I felt no different. Even though I was asking, there was no perceived assurance of receiving. So painful and agonising did this lack of assurance of salvation become, that for about 6 months I would ask again and again; always trying to say it with greater eloquence or determination. Perhaps God didn't think I was genuine! No matter what I read nor who I talked to, my heart could not be satisfied that all was well between me and God.

It wasn't that the promises of God in Scripture were unknown to me. The reality was that I did not really place my full confidence in them. I was assessing God's acceptance of me based on a self-analysis of whether I was worth accepting!

I was guessing and projecting onto God a view of how much he loved me and was willing to accept me. My feelings and self-opinion distorted the reality of who God was and how he felt about me as made clear in his word. I had to learn to place my full confidence in the promises of Scripture. In the end I wrote in a small journal entry the following:

'No matter how large or how small your doubts, examine them and remember Christ's promises. Ask yourself, 'have I done what he asked, to confess your sins and give your life to him?' If you have done these things then NO doubts can be valid ones, so get rid of them and take no notice, think about something else.'

Grace taught me how to rely on what God had said to be true even though what I felt was considerably different. Now I praise God for that period, simply because I had to learn how to wield the sword of the Spirit, the word of God. I experienced being taught by grace how to fight and stand on truth. Little did I know then, how vital this lesson was going to prove for the years ahead.

Grace to trust God's word and pray

Having discovered at first hand the mighty effect of the promises of God when applied with faith to my life, I began to apply the same principle elsewhere. If trusting God's word could bring assurance of salvation, then it was also sufficient for everything else upon which it commented. If I knew what God was like and what he had promised and I lined my life up behind these truths, then not only would I live well, but I would also be enabled to know God better and serve him more effectively.

The first summer after grasping this principle, I rose early every day, sometimes with the sun. I could not wait to read the Bible and meditate on the words and verses within. I worked my way through books of the Bible that emphasised God's nature and character and also themes that offered knowledge and insight into how he viewed me and what he had personally promised. I spent lots of time in the Psalms, Proverbs and prophetic books like Isaiah. I would often read only a verse, write it down and make a comment, then pray it back to God. Over the months I became committed to this practice as a lifestyle and by and large I have not deviated from it since.

Prayer came more naturally once I had some fuel from scriptures. I found I could apply all sorts of promises to my situations and bring them to God, reminding him of what he had said. *'Cast all your anxiety on him because he cares for you'* (1 Peter 5:7) was one such example. This promise inspired me to press through when facing some concern or other. I would remind myself and God of a particular promise and leave my burdens with him. Verses were written down and carried around throughout the day; whenever fresh waves of new anxiety dawned, I quickly fumbled in pocket to find and apply them.

Fallen at the first fence

I wish I could say I sailed through the early years of my Christian life without any failure, but this would not be true. The truth is I was saved into a church environment where few others had any zeal for the Lord. Church services were really quite dreadful in terms of there being little connection with my wavelength as a new Christian.

Teaching was sparse and no contexts existed for discipleship. I was alone and felt weighed down with no one to really talk to. I struggled to keep my zeal as all my non-Christian friends began to discover the delights of the world. More and more I became drawn into what they were doing and gave myself to things I should not have. But constantly accompanying me was a guilty conscience that would not allow anything sinful to be enjoyed.

Thankfully after a few months, two or three other people my age began to attend church (I ended up marrying one of them!) and things began to change. From this small number, a flourishing youth work and then a considerable move of the Holy Spirit developed. Over the next few years, the church changed beyond recognition. In the end we had to plant a new church, as the strains with those who wanted to keep it how it was, became completely unworkable.

What did those months of backsliding teach me? I had come to learn my frailty even as a saved child of God. Even though there were times when I felt really strong spiritually and that I could take on the world for Jesus, I had now become aware of being a very frail creature completely reliant on God to keep me. I needed his grace then every day and today is still the same. Conversely, I have also learned from my time of sinful failure, that when I feel weak and frail, guilty and useless, I can once again become strong in his strength. Grace is always available to clean and restore me.

Living with pain, growing through pain

The world we live in, and certainly in the West, constantly informs us of what we need, have a right to and deserve. Holidays, money, housing, health, friends, happiness and all problems can be solved and we can pay our way out of anything (even if it is with a credit card of debt).

After a few years of marriage my wife, who is one of the people I admire most in the world, developed what became a serious, chronic back condition. Many years have since followed of facing daily battles with often high pain levels and of living with loss. She has had to come to terms, as indeed I have, with not having the things that previously were taken for granted. Daily tasks such as cooking and cleaning usually require help; indeed every aspect of our lives has been affected. However, the loss of independence has proved most difficult: having to rely so much on family members and friends for assistance.

It is no longer possible to go on a long walk and any form of travel brings restrictions. In the course of ministry, I have visited so many countries: from the frozen beauty of Finland and the splendour of Canada; through Ukraine and the great cities of Europe; to Kenya, the USA and the golden beaches of Hawaii. I would have loved to take her with me to even just one of these places, to experience them and spend time with the believers I have been so privileged to meet. Sadly she has had to stay at home every time, and thus has served in a greater way than me, through a sacrificial willingness to release me to go and serve others.

It is right to celebrate mighty healings with wonder and gratitude. Praying for the sick and those in pain is one of my key areas to develop and persevere with, as nothing quite touches the joy experienced when I see someone's suffering end. What we as Christians often fail to do though, is honour and celebrate those who have not as yet been healed. These dear people live through their ordeals without any shred of bitterness or anger. Instead of contemplating what they will do for God when they are healed, they say 'I am alive now, today and not healed; I will serve and love him now for he is worthy'.

If you are such a person, who has had to endure long-term struggles with any kind of pain or suffering, then will know only too well the drawn-out journey of applying the grace of God. Every day you are faced with a daily choice to make and this will continue, sometimes with no prospect of release.

My testimony is that through such a pathway God has wrought considerable work in both me and my wife by our applying his grace into our lives. We have a sense of closeness with him that perhaps we wouldn't have if our circumstances were different. I cannot quite trace how this has come about but somehow we know something of what it is to *'share in his sufferings'*. (Romans 8:17)

Drawing on grace in times of great restriction when there are no answers or solutions, and indeed may never be this side of eternity, does require grace to draw on grace.

Grace in serving God

I have been in church leadership of one sort or another now for many years and have come to fully appreciate Paul's reflection in 1 Corinthians 15:10:

'But by the grace of God I am what I am, and his grace toward me was not in vain. On the contrary, I worked harder than any of them, though it was not I, but the grace of God that is with me'.

Although grace helps us to work hard, Paul saw that nothing could be achieved without God. Grace gave him the right perspective on what was God's responsibility and what was his.

1 Corinthians 3:6: *'I planted, Apollos watered, but God gave the growth.'*

Grace is given to empower us to carry out what we are called to do. Sometimes it enables us to achieve beyond what we would have imagined possible. Leaders fall into trouble when they mix up who is responsible for what. I must own up to occasionally having to learn this one myself!

God makes things grow and we are therefore stewards of what he creates. Adam and Eve were meant to steward and develop what God had created. They could not create anything but they were supposed to work hard and have vision to be fruitful and multiply what God was bringing to birth.

I have found that trusted friends who are in partnership with me in mission are a huge source of wisdom and strength. They are in themselves channels of the grace of God. Any leadership development program that teaches leaders to remain a bit distant from those they are leading, blocks one of the chief ways God provides grace. I have so often asked advice, talked through problems, laughed, planned, consulted and been much better informed. I have been warned, exhorted, encouraged and generally been made to feel alive through the relationships God has given me in church life and especially in co-workers. These relationships are indeed a major stream of God's grace.

No wonder Paul uttered to his compatriots in Romans 15:32 'So that by God's will I may come to you with joy and be refreshed in your company.' He understood that being with others whom he loved and trusted and who felt likewise about him would be refreshing.

There are times when we need solitude and to get alone with God and the Bible. There are also times when this is the last thing to do! We need people, who can 'refresh' us. I often lack wisdom to know what I need. The people who tell me are usually those who both know and love me!

Conclusion

Grace; it is all of grace. I genuinely hope you feel somewhat strengthened and freshly motivated to pursue the mighty oceans of God's grace for yourself. What I have experienced is like running down onto the beach in front of my house and filling an egg cup from the sea, only to conclude the contents are the sea itself! God's grace in any one of our lives is real and genuine but still only the outer fringes of his limitless resource of grace.

He can out-give us, out-know us, and forgive us more than we think we deserve – and more than we actually do deserve (which is usually even more). He can provide and care and move all sorts of mountains for the outworking of his ends and purposes in your life. He faces no challenge to restrict the grace he gives, or the supply you need. Yet he applies wisdom and care in each application. Not one seed is carelessly scattered as if he were someone not watching or caring little where it falls. He is the one to whom all praise is due for the gracious dealings in your life and mine.

References

1   Spurgeon, CH. Morning and Evening. Date and original publisher unknown

2   Bonar, AA, 2005. The Biography of Robert Murray McCheyne. Available from: www.shatteringdenial.com/books/the_biography_of_robert_murray_mcheyne.pdf

3   Bunyan, J. Source unknown

4   Empedocles. Available from: www.dictionary-quotes.com

5   McCheyne, RM. Cited by Tindall. J. Affinity Ministers' Fraternal Study Guide. Available from: www.affinity.org.uk/downloads/publications/study_guides/09.pdf

6   Mathews, MM,1951. A Dictionary of Americanisms on Historical Principles. Chicago: University of Chicago Press

7   American Independence Party (2009) Daily Blessing – Quoted from Charles Spurgeon's Faiths Checkbook. Available from: www.aipnews.com/talk/forums/thread-view.asp?tid=6534&posts=1&start=1

8   Precept Austin, 2010. A Primer on Biblical Meditation, Quoted from I Will Meditate My Precepts from Spurgeon's Morning and Evening. Available from: www.preceptaustin.org/a_primer_on_meditation.htm

9   Rozalowsky, A, 2009. Packer's Definition of, Purpose for, and Effect of Meditation. Quoted From Knowing God. Available from: http://alivingsacrificetogod.blogspot.com/2009/06/packers-definition-of-purpose-for-and.html

10 Precept Austin, 2010. A Primer on Biblical Meditation. Quoted from No Fast Food in the Bible. Available from: www.preceptaustin.org/a_primer_on_meditation.htm

11 McCheyne, RM. Bible Reading Calendar. Available from: web.ukonline.co.uk/d.haslam/mccheyne/calendar/calendar.pdf

12 Bonar, AA, 2005. The Biography of Robert Murray M'Cheyne, EBook #1525, p.16. Available from: www.shatteringdenial.com/books/the_biography_of_robert_murray_mcheyne.pdf

13 Beattie, FR, 2008. The Means of Grace; Prayer. Chapter XXVII, The Presbyterian Standards. Westminster Shorter Catechism Project. Available from: www.shortercatechism.com/resources/beattie/wsc_be_098-107.html